The Math Teacher's Toolbox

How to Teach Math to Teenagers and Survive

Nicholas J. Rinaldi

ROWMAN & LITTLEFIELD EDUCATION
A division of
ROWMAN & LITTLEFIELD PUBLISHERS, INC.
Lanham • New York • Toronto • Plymouth, UK

Published by Rowman & Littlefield Education
A division of Rowman & Littlefield Publishers, Inc.
A wholly owned subsidiary of The Rowman & Littlefield Publishing Group, Inc.
4501 Forbes Boulevard, Suite 200, Lanham, Maryland 20706
www.rowman.com

10 Thornbury Road, Plymouth PL6 7PP, United Kingdom

British Library Cataloguing in Publication Information Available

Library of Congress Cataloging-in-Publication Data Available

ISBN 978-1-4758-0353-2 (cloth : alk. paper) — ISBN 978-1-4758-0354-9 (pbk. : alk. paper) — ISBN 978-1-4758-0355-6 (electronic)

Printed in the United States of America

Contents

Preface

When I was in college, I took a course in psychology, which was team taught by two professors. I don't remember their names, but let's call them Professor Snooze and Professor Dynamo. Professor Snooze stood at a podium and spoke in a monotone voice. She showed no enthusiasm or energy, and if she had smiled, her face would have cracked. She knew the material, but she taught directly out of the book. There were no interactions with the students, just a straight 90-minute lecture . . . zzzzzzz.

One day, at the end of a lecture, she said, "Class is over; you are dismissed." Not one of the 200 students moved; we were all asleep or in a semiconscious state. There was one redeeming quality about her lectures; I used to record them, and on a night when I couldn't fall asleep, I would play back the lecture and slumber came instantly!

The teacher who cotaught the course was as opposite as could be. Professor Dynamo paced up and down the aisles with a handheld microphone as she vigorously presented the material. Her voice was energetic, and her lessons were vibrant.

On one occasion she was discussing Sigmund Freud and the Oedipal complex. She asked, "Here's a teenage boy whose father had passed away. Now what do you think this boy was feeling?" One student responded, "Sadness." "Not this particular boy," she said. "Maybe he was indifferent," another student replied. "Stronger!" countered Professor Dynamo. "Perhaps he was glad" yet another student suggested. "Even stronger!" the professor shouted. When no one offered a reply, Professor Dynamo bellowed, "The boy wanted his father dead so that he could have his mother!" "Bullsh*t!!" responded a student sitting in the next row.

Now, perhaps this response was not appropriate in a classroom, especially back in the mid-1960s, but it illustrates the impact this teacher had on us. We were actively engaged in the lesson, we were willing and eager to respond, and we were learning.

Most teachers have a style somewhere between those of Professor Snooze and Professor Dynamo. In a perfect world, wouldn't all teachers be more like the latter than the former? As a math teacher, it's difficult to imagine that saying, "Therefore, students, $x = 5$" would elicit the response given by the student mentioned above. However, it would be rewarding to know that your students are ready to respond because they are actively involved in the lesson.

Obviously, there are few if any topics in the traditional math curriculum that are controversial, and certainly none as provocative as the Oedipal complex. So, as math teachers, can we consistently get students actively involved in lessons covering the traditional mathematics curriculum? The answer is a resounding "Yes!"

My name is Nick Rinaldi, and for 41 years I taught mathematics at Branford High School. Branford is a town on the southern Connecticut shoreline about 10 miles east of New Haven. I am now retired from teaching in Branford and am currently an adjunct math professor at the University of New Haven (UNH). Also, for six years I taught an education course at UNH called Math Strategies in Secondary Education. This is a course for graduate students who are preparing to become math teachers. The course focuses on various teaching strategies and classroom management skills.

For the last 28 of my 41 years at Branford High School, I was the Math Department chairman. Part of my job was to go into classrooms and observe teachers as they presented their lessons.

Consequently, I worked closely with dozens of educators who displayed various levels of competency and classroom management skills. I saw a lot of good teaching along with a considerable amount of mediocre and, sometimes, even poor teaching. I noticed that, as a result, too many students were turned off to math because of the way lessons were presented. A traditional approach usually does not motivate students or enhance their learning, especially for those students who don't like math.

During my teaching career I also attended numerous conferences, workshops, and conventions. From my experiences at these meetings, my personal work with teachers, reading many articles in various educational journals, and feedback from students, I came to the conclusion that ineffective classroom management is most likely the major reason teachers struggle or even fail.

Because you are reading this book, I assume you are a middle school or high school math teacher or someone who is enrolled in a teacher preparation program. The primary objective of this book, therefore, is to provide you with various tools to help improve your classroom management skills, and as a result, to raise the interest level of your students and improve their learning.

The ideas presented have been classroom tested and can be used in virtually any middle or high school classroom, although most of the activities and ideas included are geared to high school students.

Before reading this book, which contains some proven ideas, strategies, and resources to actively engage students in learning, consider the following questions:

- Do your students actively participate in the lesson?
- Do you sometimes have difficulty keeping your students on task or motivating them to do their assigned work?
- Are you concerned about using classroom time effectively?

In other words, do you want to improve your classroom management skills? The expression *classroom management* as used in this book means the intricate art (yes, teaching is an art) educators practice to control the learning environment and to keep their students on task.

Many of the strategies and suggestions for effective teaching made in this book are not based on any specific scientific studies but on my experience over four decades of teaching math, applying ideas, observing the results, and gathering and using student feedback to make adjustments and refinements.

You must decide how and when to use these concepts and materials to effectively complement your teaching philosophy and style and to meet the needs of your students.

Acknowledgements

I would like to thank my daughter, Alicia, for her input and for contributing a teenager's and student's perspective on some of the material in this book. I am particularly grateful for the support given me by my wife, Barbara, who spent many hours helping with proofreading and editing. Her suggestions and assistance were immeasurable.

Introduction

Whether you are a new or an experienced teacher, *The Math Teacher's Tool-box* provides guidance and serves as a reference book of topics, ideas, and resources.

Think of Chapter 1 as Day 1 of the school year. What is most important at that time is establishing expectations for your students for the year; therefore, this is the subject of the first chapter.

Chapter 2 is an overview of how to engage students and lays the foundation for the strategies and activities that follow in subsequent chapters. Chapter 3 is more specific in detailing how to engage your students through opening-of-class activities.

Now that the opening of the school year and how to begin class have been addressed, attention is given in Chapter 4 to "Rinaldi's Routine," a complete and effective system for conducting a more student-centered classroom.

The topics in Chapters 5 through 10 are intended to help you actively involve your students in learning. Included are conducting inquiry-based lessons, infusing problems from the students' world into the curriculum, incorporating humor in the classroom, using the graphing calculator, reading and writing activities, and using classroom competitions to enhance learning and have fun. Most of these topics can be implemented within the framework of Rinaldi's Routine.

Chapter 11 presents several purposeful ways to close a class, and Chapter 12 contains strategies, ideas, and techniques not previously mentioned in the book that have been successfully used in the classroom and that can help to increase your effectiveness as a teacher.

The Appendix contains various forms and materials that supplement many of the topics presented. These items and many discussed in the book are easily reproducible and ready to use, thus saving you time.

Chapter One

On Your Marks, Get Set

Establishing Expectations

This chapter explains how to effectively begin a course by establishing expectations and introducing your classroom rules and procedures. Also included is a process that allows your students to write their own goals and later evaluate how well they did in attaining them.

At the beginning of each course, it is important for you to tell your students your expectations for them as well as the classroom procedures you will follow. One way to do this is through a printed course description (syllabus) that you can hand out to students on the first day of class. This course description can also be made available to students (and parents) on the school's web site or on your own web site. A sample of a syllabus is included in this chapter.

At my former school, the mathematics department developed the practice of writing course descriptions to help establish consistency within each course and to help teachers with classroom management. If the students are told up front what expectations the teacher has of them, they are more likely to comply.

To begin the process of writing course descriptions, all teachers who were teaching the same course—geometry, for example—got together to decide what the major components of the course description should be. It was then determined which components should have the same descriptions, to maintain consistency in the course, and which should vary from teacher to teacher to allow for different teaching styles and philosophies.

Each course description was entered as a template on the shared data drive on the computers. In the course description below, the first five components are the same for *all* geometry teachers. The descriptions for the last

1

four components were left blank. Each teacher filled in these spaces based on his or her teaching style and philosophy.

Below is a model of a course description.

GEOMETRY: COURSE DESCRIPTION

School Mission Statement

The mission of our school is to foster academic and personal excellence. To this end, we join with the home and community to cultivate skills, attitudes, and talents that will prepare our graduates not only to succeed in college and careers but also to become informed, responsible citizens who respect diversity, value lifelong learning, and lead fulfilling lives.

Learner Outcomes

Upon completion of this course, the student should be able to

- use mathematical reasoning in problem solving
- communicate mathematically

Course Content

A study of geometry develops spatial visualization and ability in using the deductive method. Topics include, but are not limited to, inductive and deductive reasoning, angles, triangles, quadrilaterals, polygons, circles, transformations, parallel and perpendicular lines, congruent and similar figures, right-triangle trigonometry, area, perimeter, volume, and coordinate geometry.

Course Specific Learning Goals

Upon completion of the course, students should be able to

- effectively use appropriate tools including, but not limited to, rulers, protractors, compasses, calculators, and computers to help discover and understand geometric concepts
- form conjectures and draw conclusions
- give a convincing argument to support or reject conjectures
- solve real-world problems involving geometric concepts
- see the relationship between geometry and the world in which they live

Instructional Strategies

Students will learn from

- direct instruction from the teacher
- classroom discourse including both student-to-teacher and student-to-student interaction
- discovery by the student through such means as hands-on activities and classroom experiments
- work with calculators and computers
- cooperative learning

Assessments

Assessments may include tests, quizzes, activities, labs, projects, and homework.

Grading Policy

- *Tests* count 100 points. Tests are listed on the assignment sheets (see chapter 12), so you will know well in advance when they are coming.
- *Quizzes* will be both announced and unannounced. You are also subject to notebook quizzes, in which you may use your notebooks, so keep your assignments and notes up to date. Quizzes will vary in value (10 points, 20 points, etc.)
- Some *activities* will be graded; values will vary.
- *Homework* will be spot-checked (I am looking for effort). Missed assignments due to lack of effort may be made up (although not for full credit). Missed assignments due to legal absence may be made up (for full credit) and should be shown to me as soon as possible. *If there is work to be shown, you must show it to receive full credit*; answers alone are *not* sufficient. Homework will count 10 percent of your quarter grade.
- In this course there will be a *midterm* and a *final exam*; the midterm will count as 10 percent of the first semester grade, and the final will count as 10 percent of the second semester grade.
- Your *quarter average* will be determined by dividing the amount of points you have earned by the amount of points possible.
- *Extra credit* can be earned in a variety of ways, which I will explain as the course proceeds.
- Your *semester grade* will be determined by the following formula: $S = (2Q1 + 2Q2 + \text{Midterm Exam})/5$.
- Your *final grade* will be determined by the following formula: $F = (5S + 2Q3 + 2Q4 + \text{Final Exam})/10$.

Attendance Policy

The attendance policy in this class will be identical to that stated in the student handbook.

Field Trips and Student Activities

When you miss class due to involvement in a field trip or student activity, you are responsible for what goes on in class! I suggest that you consult with me or look at the assignment sheet a few days before the activity to find out what you will be missing. You should then look over the material to determine whether you need to be in class or whether you feel you can handle the topic(s) on your own. Once you have done that, then you can make an intelligent decision as to whether or not you should miss class. When you return to class on the following day, you will be expected to have your completed homework and will be expected to take any test or quiz given that day.

Make-Up Procedures

- If you are legally absent and miss a test, quiz, or other assessment, it is your responsibility to see me to arrange to take a make-up. It is wise to make up missed work as soon as possible. Make-ups can be done during the school day or after school. Work not made up in a timely manner will be scored a *zero*.
- If your absence from class is *not* legal, you may *not* make up the work and a *zero* will be recorded as your grade. Don't let this happen to you!
- You may *retake* one test (to attempt to improve upon a poor score) per quarter subject to the following conditions:

  1. The retake must be taken no more than *five* school days after the corrected, original test was returned.
  2. The highest score you can earn is *70*.
  3. If the retake score is *lower* than the original score, the *retake score will count* (make corrections on your test and seek any help you need *before* the retake).
  4. If you received a zero for an assignment on the material leading up to the test, it must be made up and shown to me on or before the day of the original test.
  5. If you received more than one zero, you will *not* be eligible for a retake.

Behavioral Expectations

You can expect *me* to

- come to class on time and prepared for the lesson
- treat you and your classmates with respect
- treat you as an individual (we are all different)
- attempt to provide a comfortable environment conducive to learning
- explain the mathematical concepts to the best of my ability
- help you to learn how to learn
- help you to learn how to work cooperatively with others
- attempt to make the class informative, interesting, and enjoyable
- help to prepare you for the CAPT and the PSAT/SAT
- make myself available for extra help (see me to make arrangements)

You are expected to

- come to class on time
- respect the rights of the other people in your class
- come to class prepared with your textbook, homework, notebook, writing utensil, calculator, and other materials
- pay attention when someone else is speaking
- be on task during presentations, discussions, and individual and group activities
- make a valid attempt to understand the mathematics
- seek help when your individual effort and group work are not succeeding.

Students who do not consistently comply with these expectations will meet with me to discuss the problem and possible solutions.

We are now living in a world that is more technologically advanced than ever before. A strong background in mathematics will help you to function more effectively in this world. Consequently, I strongly suggest that you take as many math courses as you can.

As a long-term goal, I encourage you to become the best math student you are capable of being. As a short-term goal, my objective is to help you to be a better math student at the end of this course than you are right now—how much better is really up to you! I am looking forward to working with you. Set your goals and work hard to attain them. I am here to help you in any way I can.

GETTING OFF TO A GOOD START

Once you have discussed the course description (syllabus) and explained the classroom procedures and rules and the consequences for violators, establish a clear reminder of the basic behavioral expectations for students. Keep these rules concise, realistic, and easy to understand. You can make them poster size and display them in a place in the room where all can see.

Below is an example of rules that can be posted in the classroom.

Classroom Rules

- Respect the rights of others
- Come to class prepared: bring your book, pencil, calculator, homework, and the like
- Come to class on time

Remember, any rules you establish must be consistently enforced, or they will have little or no effect on student behavior. Also, if you do not enforce the rules or enforce them inconsistently, you are likely to lose credibility in the eyes of the students.

Student Goals

On the first day the class meets, ask students to write their personal goals. Writing their goals forces the students to think in specific terms. They are also establishing a record of what they are trying to accomplish. Having their goals in writing increases the chances of their meeting them. For an overall goal and a quarter goal, encourage the students not to write something vague such as, "I will do well." Instead, encourage students to use a letter grade because it is precise. When the quarter ends they know whether or not they have achieved their goals.

Besides writing their goals, ask students to write three strategies they will use to attain that goal, such as the following:

- I will do all my homework assignments.
- I will pay attention in class.
- I will laugh at the teacher's jokes.
- I will seek extra help when needed.

After the students fill in the first section (see the model below), you can collect the papers, read them, and put them in a file. From time to time you may want to review the goals and talk to some students to remind them of their goals and check on their progress toward achieving them. (Each student could also be given a copy of the goal statement.)

At the end of the first quarter, the goal statements are passed back to the students. Now ask them to evaluate how well they did what they said they would do to achieve their goals. They can evaluate themselves by placing the appropriate symbol next to each strategy they listed, using the following code:

+ I did a good to excellent gob.
√ I did a fair to good job.
− I did a poor job.
0 I didn't do it at all.

After they have completed their self-evaluation, the students are to write their goals and strategies to achieve them for the second quarter, and the papers are recollected. The process is repeated at the beginning of the third and fourth quarters.

Following this procedure is beneficial to students, and the goals and self-evaluations provide insight to their parents. You can use these papers during parent conferences. Most parents enjoy reading what their son or daughter wrote, and their goals, learning strategies, and self-evaluations are often the basis for a meaningful discussion with the students' parents.

A sample form is given on the next page.

My Goals

Name_____ Date_____ Course_____ Period___

My overall goal in this course is_____.

My goal for the first quarter is_____.

In order to attain this goal, I will

    1. _____
    2. _____
    3. _____

My goal for the second quarter is_____.

In order to attain this goal, I will

    1. _____
    2. _____
    3. _____

My goal for the third quarter is_____.

In order to attain this goal, I will

    1. _____
    2. _____
    3. _____

My goal for the fourth quarter is_____.

In order to attain this goal, I will

    1. _____
    2. _____
    3. _____

Establishing expectations and classroom rules, writing and discussing your course description, and having students write their goals are all aspects of a positive beginning of a school year or course. These strategies are effective in getting the students engaged in the course at the outset and lead into the next topic of getting the students actively involved.

Chapter Two

Put Me In, Coach

Getting Students Actively Involved

Active involvement of students is essential for successful classroom management. This chapter provides an overview for engaging students and lays the foundation for the strategies and activities that follow in subsequent chapters.

As you know, the attention span of adolescents is very short. The teacher who talks *at* his or her students for long periods of time (like Professor Snooze, who was mentioned in the preface) usually is not effectively managing his or her classroom.

In an effective classroom, the teacher usually changes activities several times but keeps transition time (time between activities) to a minimum; this is accomplished by careful planning. For example, transition time is minimal if the teacher clearly explains the procedure to be followed in the next activity *before* passing out materials, which may distract the students from paying attention.

The following strategies and activities have been shown to be valuable tools for effective classroom management:

- Opening-of-class activities
- Cooperative learning
- Inquiry-based/discovery lessons
- Problems in the students' world
- Use of humor
- Use of technology
- Reading and writing in the math class
- Classroom competitions
- Closing activities

Each is addressed in the pages that follow.

If you are going to develop and maintain good classroom management skills, it is very important that you teach a varied lesson and make every attempt to keep students on task. The topics listed above should help. But please keep in mind that no matter what you do, there may still be some students who take little or no responsibility for their own learning and may be very difficult to reach. The following true story illustrates that point.

While a math teacher was presenting a lesson, he noticed a student whose focus was clearly elsewhere. Later the student admitted that he didn't understand the material, but he assertively stated that it wasn't his fault. He looked the teacher squarely in the eye and said, "You shouldn't be explaining something when I'm not paying attention."

Chapter Three

Ladies and Gentlemen, Start Your Engines

Opening-of-Class Activities

At the beginning of each class, you can stimulate the students mentally and get them ready for the lesson by giving them one of a variety of problems. This chapter describes and has models of such problems:

- Problems to introduce the next lesson
- Problems to review previous lessons
- Real-world math problems
- Holiday problems
- SAT prep questions
- General brain teasers

At your discretion, students can be rewarded with extra credit, pencils, candy, or other prizes for successfully completing the activity.

The objectives of using opening-of-class activities are

- to get the students mentally engaged before the lesson begins
- to introduce a new lesson or review previously covered lessons
- to introduce and then be able to discuss real-world issues like nutrition, alcohol use, smoking, and so forth, topics and discussions that are not usually a part of the traditional mathematics curriculum
- to allow the weaker math students the opportunity to compete with the stronger students; the nonmathematical problems give *all* students a chance for success

• to have some fun

Below are some examples of opening-of-class activities. (Answers are at the end of the book.) You are encouraged to compile your own collection throughout your teaching career. Sharing or exchanging problems of this nature with your teaching colleagues is usually a good idea.

PROBLEMS TO INTRODUCE THE NEXT LESSON

Lesson Objective: To use inductive reasoning to make conjectures

What Comes Next?

1. 5, 9, 13, 17, _____
2. 15, 12, 9, 6, _____
3. 1, 1/2, 1/4, 1/8, _____
4. 1, 2, 4, 7, _____
5. 1, 1, 2, 3, 5, _____
6. J, F, M, A, _____
7. S, M, T, W, _____
8. F, S, T, F, _____
9. D, R, M, F, _____
10. 1, 2, _____

Challenge: AF, BE, CF, DI, FD, ___

PROBLEMS TO REVIEW A PREVIOUS LESSON

The Bottom Line

Directions: Calculate the answer to each of the problems. (Don't forget the rule for order of operations: *Please Excuse My Dear Aunt Sally* (that is, *P*arentheses, *E*xponents, *M*ultiply, *D*ivide, *A*dd, *S*ubtract). For each problem, show the three answers and the bottom line (final answer).

The value of $3x^2$ when $x = 1$

–

The value of x if $4x + 3 = 19$

*

The value of $(3x)^2$ when $x = 1$

The final answer is ___ – ___ * ___ = _____.

REAL-WORLD PROBLEMS

Up in Smoke

According to a TV ad sponsored by the American Medical Association, a cigarette smoker shortens the length of his or her life by 9 minutes for each cigarette smoked. A high school student smokes three-quarters of a pack a day (there are 20 cigarettes in a pack). He or she has been smoking for exactly three non–leap years. So far, by how many days (to the nearest day) has this student already shortened his or her life?

Five-a-Day Is the Healthy Way

According to a TV ad sponsored by the American Diabetes Association (ADA), we should all eat a healthy diet that is low in fat and sugar and high in fiber. The ADA recommends eating 5 total servings of fruits and vegetables each day.

If you were to follow their advice and ate 3 servings of veggies and 2 servings of fruit each day from January to June, and then ate 2 servings of veggies and 3 of fruit each day from July to December, how many servings of veggies would you eat in a non–leap year? (Remember: September, April, June, and November each have 30 days.)

HOLIDAY PROBLEMS

Halloween: The Witch's Broom

Little Wendy wants to dress up as a witch for Halloween. She has a very good costume but wants to add a cape and broom as accessories. The cape and broom together cost $60, and the cape costs $30 more than the broom. How much does the broom cost?

Christmas: The North Pole

Santa Claus and his reindeer leave the North Pole and fly 100 miles due south. Then they turn and fly 200 miles due east. At this point, how far are they from the North Pole?

SAT PREP QUESTIONS

There are many commercial books available to provide students with SAT practice. Your school library may have some, or you can go online to find problems. You can select several pages of problems, have them reproduced into packets, and give one to each student. (Even students who have already completed their SATs can derive benefit from this activity because of the problem-solving skills and strategies involved.)

Every few weeks instruct the students to bring their packets to class with them. The problems can be used as an opening-of-class activity. Tell the students to work a problem or two on a given page. Give them a limited amount of time to simulate the timed nature of the SAT. After the time limit is up, go over the problems, paying close attention to the type of problem-solving skill or strategy that could be used. Asking students how they solved the problem is helpful and instructive to others. Sometimes a student may suggest a clever solution that no one else considered. The entire process usually takes less than 5 minutes.

GENERAL BRAIN TEASERS

Sick Leave

Walter spent two days in the hospital. He was neither sick nor injured, but when it was time to leave he had to be carried out. Why?

A Riddle

What is black when you buy it, red when you use it, and gray when you throw it away?

Coins, Coins, Coins

Use *exactly* 50 United States coins to make change for a dollar.

Equations Investigations

Example:

- $2000 = P$ in a T
- $2000 = P$ounds in a Ton

  1. $26 = L$ of the A
  2. $12 = S$ of the Z
  3. $32 = D F$ at which W F
  4. $90 = D$ in a R A
  5. $24 = H$ in a D
  6. $29 = D$ in F in a L Y
  7. $40 = D$ and N of the G F
  8. $30 = D H S, A, J,$ and N

9. 3 = W M
10. 7 = D

Problems such as those suggested above initiate mental activity, which usually results in the students being more actively involved in the lesson that follows. Also, many students simply like doing these problems and find them an enjoyable part of the course. In addition you may find that you teach a lot of problem-solving strategies when discussing the solutions of these problems.

Now that you have done the opening-of-class activity, in which the majority of the class usually participates, you now need to proceed with the lesson and attempt to keep the students actively involved. The next chapter addresses that issue.

Chapter Four

And the Children Shall Lead

Rinaldi's Routine — Creating a
Student-Centered Classroom

Now that you have completed the opening-of-class activity, it's time to begin using classroom management skills to get and keep the students on task for the remainder of the period.

This chapter describes in detail a classroom management strategy that was developed by the author and fine-tuned over many years. It is a complete system for conducting a more student-centered classroom. Based on the author's personal observations, input from colleagues, administrators, and parents, and surveys completed by students, this approach is a very effective classroom management tool.

Most teachers, especially beginners, will identify with the following scenario. The bell rings, signifying the start of class. If an opening-of-class activity is used, it is addressed. The lesson now begins with the teacher going over the previous assignment. Let's say the homework was exercises 1 through 10 on page 97. The teacher asks, "Who had trouble with number 1?" Assume three hands go up. In a class of 25 students, that means 22 hands don't go up.

Now, should the teacher go over number 1, even though the overwhelming majority of the class "got" the problem? If the problem is not done, then the needs of those three students are not being met. If number 1 is done at the board by the teacher or another student, what do the others in the class do? Most already know how to do the problem. Then there are problems 2 through 10 to address. What should be done?

It is not uncommon for a teacher to spend the majority of class time going over homework, often to the dismay (and boredom) of those who got all the problems correct. Clearly, this system is not effective. A better method is needed.

Below is an effective system of classroom management called "Rinaldi's Routine." Its objectives are as follows:

- To help keep the students on task
- To help students learn the material
- To help students become autonomous learners
- To make the daily operation of class more time effective
- To teach the value of collaborating on problems
- To help students to improve interpersonal relationships
- To help students develop leadership skills

As you can see, many of these skills are "people skills," which are introduced in class and taught as part of the curriculum. Remember, the students you have will use most of the math skills they learn for a relatively short time, but they use the people skills for the rest of their lives.

To implement Rinaldi's Routine, begin on the second or third day of the course. On paper, arrange your students into heterogeneous cooperative learning groups based on the final grades in their previous math course. Organize the teams to be as academically balanced as possible; that is, each team should have approximately the same number of A, B, C, and D students. Strong math students are appointed to be taskmasters, one for each team.

Explain to the students the daily routine to be followed. (You will find that you have to remind the students of the procedure only once or twice thereafter before it becomes a natural part of the class.) Now tell the students the members of each team and assign seats so that team members sit close to each other. Give each taskmaster a written explanation of his or her role (see the Appendix), which you should also describe to the other students. Tell everyone that the taskmasters will be evaluated (but not graded) by team members at the end of the quarter. Also mention that virtually everyone will be a taskmaster sometime during the year.

The team's first task is to fill out a team report (see Appendix), a non-threatening information sheet asking about the students' favorite TV shows, bands, and so forth. This team profile is an "icebreaker" and allows the students to get to know each other a little better. Each team then decides upon a team name. It could be based on information from the profile or anything else they choose. The name must be agreed upon by all team members, and it may not be derogatory to any person or group; you are the judge with regards to this matter.

On a typical day, class begins with an opening activity (see Chapter 3). The activity or problem is almost always displayed on the room's white board (from an overhead projector or computer) or handwritten on the board. This is done shortly before class begins. When students enter the room, most begin working on the problem. While students are doing this, you will usually take attendance or perform some other administrative task.

After a few minutes, discuss the solution to the opening activity with the students. Then the lesson begins. If new material is to be presented, do so for the *first* part to the class, usually 15 to 30 minutes, depending on the nature of the material and the teaching strategy to be used.

Next the students begin to work in their groups going over the previous assignment. They check the answers in the back of the book. If the answers are not there, you can read them or display them on the white board.

The taskmaster now takes control of the group, asking teammates if anyone was unable to do any problems from the previous assignment. If *no one* in the group could get a certain problem, it is considered to be "undoable." If at least one student in the team was able to solve the problem, it is not considered undoable and is to be handled within the team; that is, someone in the team who solved the problem is to teach it to anyone who was unable to get a solution.

While the students are working, you can take this opportunity to walk around the room and check homework (if that is part of your classroom procedure). Once that task has been completed, float from group to group, pad and pencil in hand, asking the taskmaster for any undoables the group had.

Once you have communicated with each group and written down all the undoables, address them. If more than one team was unable to do a particular problem, write the solution on the board or display it on the board from the overhead projector or computer. With experience, you can usually anticipate which types of problems cause trouble and prepare them ahead of time. This takes some extra effort, but you then have the solutions to these problems for other classes later in the day or later in your career. It is a real classroom time saver.

After the problem is displayed, move out of the way. The hope here is that upon seeing the solution, at least one member of the team requesting help with the problem will now understand how to do it and be able to explain it to his or her teammates. This is usually what happens.

If the solution is still unclear, give a more detailed explanation at the board. If that is not sufficient, give the group(s) still having difficulty individual attention. While this is happening, any group that has finished going over the homework and has no undoables is now free to work on the next assignment, which is on an assignment sheet that you have previously given to the students at the beginning of the unit of work. (See Chapter 12.)

Before the class ends, you can provide closure by asking a student to verbally summarize the lesson, or perhaps the entire class can write down the most important concepts discussed. In some instances, an "Exit Slip" might be used. (See Chapter 11.)

You can use the procedure explained above perhaps three or four days per week throughout the quarter. Of course, it is not used on test days or during classes where something special is happening, like a Team Tournament. (See Chapter 10.)

Near the end of the quarter, teams meet for one last time. Ask each person to make at least one complimentary statement about each group member. Also, the taskmaster is evaluated by having his or her teammates fill out a special form (see Appendix) made for that purpose. The completed forms are given to the taskmaster for self-reflection and self-evaluation.

Teams are changed every quarter for two reasons. First, it is beneficial to the students to work with a variety of personalities. Second, in every class there are usually some excellent student "teachers." They should be given the opportunity to work with as many other students as possible.

For the second quarter, based on first quarter grades and other factors such as compatibility, new teams are formed, with everyone having different teammates. New taskmasters are appointed, and the procedure implemented for the first quarter is followed.

During the third quarter, new teams are again formed, although you will find it is more difficult to maintain an academic balance and not repeat teammates. The roles of taskmasters are assigned, preferably to students who have not previously had that responsibility.

During the fourth quarter, follow the procedure used during the first three quarters, or you can have the students pick their own teams and taskmasters.

Formal and informal feedback from students indicates that this routine is beneficial to the vast majority of students.

Teachers sometimes use group work as a learning strategy. Sometimes it is successful while other times it is not. For group work to be successful, many students need some type of extrinsic motivation in order to help their teammates. If students do not help each other, group work is ineffective. The motivation explained below has shown to be effective in making group work successful.

If all team members earn a score of 70 or better on the chapter test, then each is rewarded by having 3 extra-credit points added to the test score; scores of 80 or better by *all* members earn 4 extra-credit points, and scores of 90 or better earn 5 extra-credit points. The results of surveys completed by the author's students in various courses from an eight-year period (see the following sections) indicate that the possibility of earning extra credit is a strong factor motivating students to help each other.

MATHEMATICS TEAM SURVEY

(A summary of 426 responses is indicated below each item.)

Course_____ Period_____ Date_____

I am interested in your opinion regarding certain aspects of team learning in this class. Below are three statements. Please respond to each by indicating the degree with which you agree or disagree with the statement. Use the following codes:

SA means you *S*trongly *A*gree

MA means you *M*ostly *A*gree

MD means you *M*ostly *D*isagree

SD means you *S*trongly *D*isagree

Circle your choice.

The 3 to 5 extra credit points that could be added to my test score if all members of my team score 70 or better on their tests . . .

1. Motivate me to work harder to get better test scores.

SA	MA	MD	SD
209 or 49%	188 or 44%	23 or 5%	6 or 1%
93%		7%	

2. Motivate me to help my teammates to learn the material.

SA	MA	MD	SD
166 or 39%	221 or 52%	32 or 8%	7 or 2%
91%		9%	

3. Create in me anxiety or stress because I fear I will be the only one in my team *not* to score 70 or better, causing my teammates not to get extra credit.

SA	MA	MD	SD
44 or 10%	77 or 18%	168 or 39%	137 or 32%
	28%		72%

Note: Percent totals may not add up to 100 percent due to rounding.

It is important that the *cooperative learning* group method described above in Rinaldi's Routine is not confused with *simple group work*. What's the difference? Group work means students are working in groups. For simple groups to become cooperative learning groups, three elements must be present:

1. Students must be motivated extrinsically to work together (after a while, the motivation for many students becomes intrinsic). Providing some tangible reward like extra credit, candy, pencils, or other prizes is usually necessary.
2. Students must realize that the only way they can earn the reward is for each team member to be successful. They must develop a "swim or sink together" attitude.
3. Students must be periodically given the opportunity to process the degree of effectiveness at which individual members and the group are working.

To address item 3, throughout the quarter various processing forms are given to individuals or teams to complete. Basically these forms allow the students to analyze their own or the team's performance in an attempt to determine strengths and weaknesses and to develop an action plan for improvement. These forms vary in complexity. The simpler ones are used at the beginning of the course. As students become more familiar with group processing, more complex forms are used. (Several examples of processing forms can be found in the Appendix.)

The survey results below, completed by the author's students in various courses over a three-year period, indicate that overall, the cooperative-learning-based Rinaldi's Routine is very beneficial to students.

COOPERATIVE LEARNING EVALUATION

(A summary of 226 responses is given for each item)

Course_____ Period_____ Date_____

I would appreciate your help in evaluating the cooperative learning groups we have used in our classroom. Please indicate your degree of agreement or disagreement with each statement by circling the appropriate letter. Use the following codes:

SA means you *S*trongly *A*gree

MA means you *M*ostly *A*gree

MD means you *M*ostly *D*isagree

SD means you *S*trongly *D*isagree

Circle your choice.

Because of my work in cooperative learning groups . . .

1. I have learned more and retained it longer.

SA	MA	MD	SD
16%	71%	11%	1%
87%		12%	

2. I am able to reason at a higher level.

SA	MA	MD	SD
18%	60%	21%	1%
78%		22%	

3. I have a greater ability to view situations from another's perspective.

SA	MA	MD	SD
30%	51%	17%	2%
81%		19%	

4. I am more highly motivated.

SA	MA	MD	SD
23%	50%	24%	3%
73%		27%	

5. I have a more positive, accepting, and supportive relationship with my peers.

SA	MA	MD	SD
33%	58%	7%	2%
91%		9%	

6. I have a more positive attitude toward math, learning, and school.

SA	MA	MD	SD
19%	50%	27%	4%
69%		31%	

7. I have a more positive attitude toward teachers, principals, and other school personnel.

SA	MA	MD	SD
11%	50%	33%	6%
61%		39%	

8. I have higher self-esteem based on basic self-acceptance.

SA	MA	MD	SD
18%	51%	26%	5%
69%		31%	

9. I am receiving greater social support.

SA	MA	MD	SD
24%	56%	17%	2%
80%		19%	

10. I am better adjusted psychologically.

SA	MA	MD	SD
13%	51%	29%	7%
64%		36%	

11. I spend more time on task (working on the subject matter).

SA	MA	MD	SD
30%	44%	21%	5%
74%		26%	

12. I have greater collaborative skills and attitudes necessary for working effectively with others.

SA	MA	MD	SD
43%	48%	8%	1%
91%		9%	

In this chapter a system for classroom management was presented, and research was displayed showing its effectiveness. This approach transforms the usually teacher-centered classroom into one that is more student centered.

Rinaldi's Routine can be used as the framework for the various teaching strategies that follow. When and how often to use this system is up to the discretion of the classroom teacher.

Chapter Five

Eureka

Inquiry-Based and Discovery Lessons

As mentioned earlier, an important component of effective classroom management is the ability of the teacher to keep the students actively involved. This chapter has many suggestions and activities that can be used to help students to work, independently or with classmates, to discover a pattern, rule, property, theorem, or concept.

It usually takes longer for students to discover what you want them to learn, but the discovery approach gives them a feeling of accomplishment. Also, when students discover a rule, property, or concept, it appears that what they learn is retained longer than if they were told the concept or read it in a book. Also, since they are actively involved in the learning, the concept they learned is more meaningful to them.

Some discovery lessons can be very complex, taking up the entire period, while others can be done in a relatively short time. While students are discovering, you are free to walk around the room providing hints and steering students in the right direction.

Inquiry-based lessons work very well in a group setting. You may present the task to the entire class and then have them work in groups in an attempt to make a discovery. After an appropriate amount of time, call on each group and have them report to the class what discoveries they made.

Because of the amount of time needed to complete these lessons, this type of strategy cannot be used too often if you expect to get through the entire curriculum; however, a few inquiry-based or discovery lessons should be included during the quarter.

Chapter 5

DISCOVERING PATTERNS

Below is a discovery activity that can be used in virtually any class. While it may not fit precisely into any specific part the curriculum, it does allow the students to discover something on their own, a skill that will serve them well in their lives. Look for or write activities like this to add to your own toolbox.

Checkerboard Squares

The question is: *How many squares are there on a checkerboard?*

The answer most commonly given is "64," based on the fact that there are eight squares along each edge. However, you must consider that there are some 2 × 2 squares on the board, and some 3 × 3 squares, and so on. So, what is the total number of squares on a checkerboard?

In general, one of the objectives of mathematics is to get you to make predictions from data you have collected—predictions that can be later justified by a reasonable argument or a formal proof. So, to answer the question, you can begin by considering a checkerboard that is 1 × 1, and then one that is 2 × 2, and then one that is 3 × 3, and so forth. Collect the data in a chart or table and look for a pattern. When you think you see one, predict the number of squares on the next-larger board and test it. If your prediction is correct, you can complete the chart and then answer the original question.

Extensions

After you have found the number of squares on an 8 × 8 checkerboard, can you predict how many squares there are on a 9 × 9, or 10 × 10, or $n \times n$ checkerboard? Then consider a three-dimensional checkerboard. Can you predict how many cubic blocks are there in a 4 × 4 × 4 cube, or a 5 × 5 × 5 cube, or an $n \times n \times n$ cube?

The extensions given above could provide differentiated instruction for students who have the interest, skill, and motivation. The extensions could also be given as an extra-credit project.

DISCOVERING CONCEPTS

Because most students do not have much experience with discovery, it is probably wise if you precede inquiry-based lessons by asking questions that require students to experiment to discover the answers. These questions usually work well in a group setting. The students have the opportunity to experiment with a variety of values before reaching a conclusion. They then can discuss or argue their points of view among themselves before sharing their findings with the rest of the class. For example, you might ask,

- Which is greater, x or $-x$?
- When, if ever, is $(1/x) > x$?
- When, if ever, is the square root of $x > x$?
- If $x^2 = y^2$, does $x = y$?
- When, if ever, does $(x + 1)^2 = x^2 + 1$?
- When, if ever, is $x > x^2$?
- If the sides of a rectangle are doubled, what effect does that have on the perimeter? On the area?

Once students have had some experience discovering small things, they may be ready to proceed to discovering larger concepts. You can take a straightforward presentation in the textbook and give it to the students in the form of an inquiry-based lesson. It may take a little time to prepare this lesson, but it is time well spent.

The following is a small sample of topics suitable for inquiry-based lessons:

- Rate $\times$ time = distance
- The laws of exponents
- The rule for changing the direction of the "greater than" or "less than" sign when solving inequalities
- Properties of radicals
- The formulas for the nth term and sum of arithmetic and geometric sequences
- Why the graph of a linear function is a line
- Why the graph of a quadratic function is a parabola
- The area of a rectangle
- Why the sum of the angle measures in a triangle is 180 degrees

- The Pythagorean theorem

A graphing calculator may be useful for the following discoveries:

- The functions of *m* and *b* in the graph of $y = mx + b$
- The functions of *a*, *h*, and *k* in the graph of $y = a(x - h)^2 + k$
- The functions of *a*, *b*, *c*, and *d* in the graph of $a \times \sin(bx - c) + d$

Below are some sample inquiry-based lessons.

Chapter 5

Algebra: Properties of Exponents

Objective: to develop rules for working with exponents; more specifically, how do we simplify the following expressions?

$x^a \times x^b$

$(x^a)^b$

Consider the expression 2^3. Recall that 2 is called the base and 3 is called the exponent. 2^3 means $2 \times 2 \times 2$ because the exponent tells us how many times the base is used as a factor. Now what happens if we multiply $2^3 \times 2^4$? Which, if any, of the following answers is correct?

(a) 2^{12} (b) 2^7 (c) 4^{12} (d) 4^7

Consider the answers on your own or with a partner. After 2 to 3 minutes I will call on someone for their conclusion.

1. Now, simplify $x^a \times x^b$

   Next consider $(2^3)^2$. Does this equal 2^5, 2^6, 2^9, or something else?

   Again, work on your own or with a partner to answer the question. After a short time I will call on someone for his or her conclusion.

2. Now, simplify $(x^a)^b$

Once the formulas for questions 1 and 2 have been correctly discovered, traditional problems applying these formulas can now be assigned from the textbook or worksheet. The remaining laws of exponents can be handled using the discovery approach later in the class or in the days that follow.

This lesson accomplishes two things: (1) the students discover for themselves the rules they will need to use when working with exponents, and (2) telling them that someone will be called on in a few minutes increases the chances of more students doing the activity.

There are many opportunities for discovery in a geometry class. Below is one example.

Geometry: The Triangle Angle-Sum Theorem

Name_____ Period _____

1. Using a ruler, draw a large scalene triangle (no two sides congruent).
2. Number the angles 1, 2, and 3. Place each number *inside* the triangle close to the vertex.
3. With your protractor, carefully measure each angle and record the measurements. What is the *sum* of the measurements? _____ Compare your results with those sitting near you.
4. Now cut out the triangle and then tear off all three angles. Place the angles adjacent to each other (vertices touching) to form one large angle. Does this part of the activity support the conclusion you reached in step 3? _____ Explain.

5. Using a complete sentence, write a conjecture about the sum of the measures of the angles of a triangle.

Inquiry-based lessons for elementary algebra and geometry classes are relatively easy to write and implement. Such lessons for more advanced classes are usually more intricate and require a greater effort to create.

Below are two discovery lessons that can be used in an advanced algebra class; they could also probably be used in some algebra II classes and in precalculus classes. They require the use of a graphing calculator. (Please note that the instructions for each of the problems are written for the TI-83/ TI-83+ or the TI-84/TI-84+. If a different calculator is used, adjustments may have to be made.)

Parabolas from Data

Objective: To use given data to find the equation of a parabola and draw its graph using the graphing calculator

(1) x	-1	0	1	2	3
f(x)	-1	0	3	8	15

Figure 5.1

- Begin by going to [STAT]; then edit, then [ENTER].
- Clear any data that is currently in the table by moving the cursor onto L1, then press [CLEAR], then [ENTER]. Then move your cursor to L2 and press [CLEAR], then [ENTER].
- Enter the *x* values from Figure 5.1 in L1 and the *y* values in L2. After each entry hit [ENTER].
- Hit [2nd] [MODE] to return to the home screen.
- Clear the *y*= menu by hitting [Y=] then [CLEAR].
- If necessary (look at the data you are given), adjust the window by hitting [WINDOW] and adjusting the Xmin, Xmax, Ymin, and Ymax.

To get a scatter plot:

- Hit [2nd] [Y=], then [1], go to ON, and hit [ENTER].
- For type: go to the first chart—that is, the scatter plot—and hit [ENTER].
- Make sure the Xlist states L1 and the Ylist states L2.
- Go to Mark and choose the mark you want to show on the scatter plot, and hit [ENTER].
- Hit [GRAPH].

When you get your plot, does it look like you expected? Is all your information there? If not, go to [WINDOW] and make any necessary adjustments.

To find the equation of the line of best fit:

- Hit [STAT], then move to CALC. Bring the cursor down to the appropriate regression (in this case it is QuadReg) and hit [ENTER].
- On your screen you should have QuadReg. Now hit [2nd] [1] [,] [2nd] [2] [,] [VARS], move to Y-VARS, and hit [1] [1] [ENTER].
- [Y=] will give you the equation of the line.
- [GRAPH] will graph the line.

Using the graphing calculator, find the equations and sketch the graphs for the data representing a quadratic function. See Figure 5.2. State the coordinates of the vertex of each parabola.

(2) x	-1	0	1	2	3
f(x)	6	3	2	3	6
(3) x	-1	0	1	2	3
f(x)	12	7	4	3	4
(4) x	-1	0	1	2	3
f(x)	9	3	1	3	9
(5) x	-1	0	1	2	3
f(x)	7	4	5	10	19

Figure 5.2

Polynomial Functions: End Behavior

A polynomial function is formed by adding or subtracting power functions and constants. The general standard form of a polynomial function is
$$f(x) = ax^n + bx^{n-1} + cx^{n-2} + \ldots + gx^2 + hx + k.$$
For example, $g(x) = 2x^4 + 5x^3 - 3x^2 + 4x + 1$.

The terms in the polynomials above are in descending order by degree. The exponent in a term determines the degree of that term. The highest degree of any term determines the degree of the polynomial. For example, from above, $f(x)$ has degree n, and $g(x)$ has degree 4.

The *end behavior* of a graph describes the far left and far right portions of the graph. The graphs of polynomial functions show four types of end behavior: *up and up*, *down and down*, *down and up*, and *up and down*.

Up and Up   Down and Down   Down and Up   Up and Down
$$(\uparrow \uparrow)(\downarrow \downarrow)(\downarrow \uparrow)(\uparrow \downarrow)$$

Work alone or with one or more partners. On the graphing calculator, draw the graphs of each of the polynomial functions below to determine the end behavior. Look for patterns. Draw some conclusions that will allow you to determine end behavior simply by looking at the equation of the function.

1. $f(x) = 4x^2 - 3$
2. $f(x) = -x^3 + 5x$
3. $f(x) = -3x^4 + 3x$
4. $f(x) = 2x^6 - 3$
5. $f(x) = x^5 + x$
6. $f(x) = -2x^3 + x$
7. $f(x) = -x^4 + 3x$
8. $f(x) = 2x^3 - 4x$
9. $f(x) = x^6 - 2x$
10. $f(x) = -x^5 + x$

In this chapter, several suggestions and activities were given to help students to discover a pattern, rule, property, theorem, or concept. At first, you may feel uncomfortable using inquiry-based lessons. However, after you have done a few, you will feel more at ease with this strategy. Remember, an important part of effective classroom management is to get your students actively involved. This type of lesson does just that.

Chapter Six

"When Will I Ever Use This?"

Problems in the Students' World

Students sometimes ask, "What good is this stuff?" or, "When will I ever use this?" or, "How does what I'm learning apply to my life?" Whenever possible, you should try to incorporate into the classroom problems from the students' world. These problems are meaningful to the students and, consequently, students are more likely to take interest in them and work harder at finding a solution.

This type of problem often asks the students to deal with a personal aspect of their lives or to use their own bodies to collect and use data. For example, if the class is doing a unit on mean, mode, and median, instead of using data from the textbook, you could have the students collect personal data to answer questions like "What is the average number of heartbeats per minute for the students in this room? What is the mode? What is the median?"

Before beginning, it is usually motivational to ask students to predict the answers to the above questions. Many will eagerly do the activity to find out how close they were to the actual answers. You could even collect the predictions and reward the student(s) whose predictions came closest to the actual answer.

There are a surprising number of students who have no idea how many times their heart beats per minute and who do not understand the health issues involved. This is a good opportunity to discuss low heart rates and why they are preferable to high rates. This could lead to an informal discussion on exercise, diet, or other health issues that are beneficial to kids but are rarely, if ever, brought up in a math class.

Another example of data students seem to enjoy collecting and analyzing is the number of times students blink per minute. Asking them to find the mean, mode, and median for this common bodily function is fun for most kids. Predicting the average heart rate or the number of times students in the room blink could also be used as an opening-of-class activity.

Samples of other activities involving data from the students' world are given in the remainder of this chapter.

CIRCLE GRAPHS

Name _____ Date _____

Period _____

Below are listed activities that you perform every day. Considering only weekdays, list the approximate amount of time you normally spend on each activity. Then calculate the percentage of the day spent on that activity. Now calculate the measure of the central angle for each activity. Finally draw a circle graph representing these statistics. Label the graph appropriately.

Activity   Time (hrs.)   Percent   Measure of Central Angle

Eating

Sleeping

School

Homework

TV

Miscellaneous

Students usually find it interesting if the teacher summarizes the results and displays them on the board. This allows students to see how they compare with their classmates in regards to time spent doing the various activities. Sometimes a lively discussion can ensue.

SCALE DRAWINGS AND MORE

Part 1

Objective: This part of the assignment will help you to practice the skills of creating ratios and proportions and applying them to a real-world situation, and it provides practice in following directions.

Task: Your task is to create a scale drawing, done *by hand* (no computer), of your bedroom (or another room in your house) and three items in the room. You will use the scale 1/4 inch to 1 foot.

Materials: This sheet, your assessment sheet, your scale drawing, a ruler, a tape measure (or other measuring device), a pencil, and a marker.

Procedure:

1. Make a rough sketch of the room to record the measurements.
2. Measure the room to the nearest half foot and record the measurements on your sketch.
3. If you are making a sketch of your bedroom, measure the length and width of your bed, your dresser, and another piece of furniture, all to the nearest foot. If you are doing another room, measure the lengths and widths of three pieces of furniture in that room to the nearest half foot.
4. Using a ruler, a pencil, and a piece of blank 8-1/2" by 11" paper (no graph paper), carefully and accurately draw the room using the scale 1/4 inch to 1 foot. (The drawing should be a two-dimensional "bird's-eye" view.)
5. When your handmade drawing is complete, go back over all the lines in pen or marker. Label all the measurements to the nearest half foot (for example, 7 feet, 10.5 feet, along the walls; table: 3 feet by 2 feet, etc.) Also, label the items in the room by name.
6. (Optional) Now add your own special touches such as color, extra furniture, area rugs, and so forth.

Part 2

Objective: To review finding the area of a polygon, converting square feet into square yards, and calculating costs.

Task: Suppose you decide to install wall-to-wall carpet in this room. Your task is to calculate the cost of this carpet.

Procedure:

1. Using a search engine (Yahoo!, for example) on the computer, find a web site that sells carpet. List the address.
2. Choose a grade (quality) and style of carpet and note the cost. (Not all web sites advertising carpet give prices, so keep searching until you find one that does.)
3. Calculate the area of the room. Show your work clearly.
4. Calculate the cost of the carpet. Show your work clearly.

Part 3: Final Details

1. Write a title that describes the drawing.
2. Put your name, date, and period on the drawing.
3. Turn in this sheet and the assessment sheet.

The project is due on _____. (There will be a 10-point penalty for each day the project is late.)

SCALE DRAWINGS AND MORE ASSESSMENT SHEET

Name _____ Date _____

Period _____

	Pts. Possible	Self-Rating	Pts. Earned
Part 1			
A ratio of 1/4 inch to 1 foot was correctly used.	10	____	____
A key noting the scale is clearly labeled on the drawing.	5	____	____
The *actual* (not scale) widths and lengths of the room measurements are clearly labeled.	5	____	____
The *actual* widths and lengths of the furniture dimensions are clearly labeled.	5	____	____
Items in the room are labeled by name.	5	____	____
The drawing is neat and easy to read.	5	____	____
Part 2			
The name of the carpet web site is listed.	5	____	____
The cost of the carpet is noted.	5	____	____
The area of the room is accurately calculated in square feet.	10	____	____
The area of the room is correctly converted to square yards.	5	____	____
The cost is accurately calculated.	5	____	____
Part 3			
This assessment sheet was turned in.	5	____	____
Directions were followed (title, name, date, period).	5	____	____
Overall appearance is satisfactory.	5	____	____
Late penalty (−10 points per day late)		____	____
TOTAL	*80*	____	____

THE MEANEST KIDS IN SCHOOL

The activity that follows involves real data from the students' world. This project is fun for the students (and the teacher).

Begin by giving the sheets below to every math teacher in the school, one copy for each of their classes. (Math teachers are usually more receptive to doing this than are non–math teachers.) If most teachers participate, there will be a reasonably good sample.

To: Math Teachers
From:
Date:

One of my math classes is studying statistics. We would appreciate your help in collecting data to determine the "meanest" (most average with reference to height, weight, and age) boy and girl in the freshman, sophomore, junior, and senior classes in our high school. Kindly fill in your name, the class, and period on the attached sheets and then circulate them among members of your classes, asking them to provide the information requested. *Participation is voluntary.*

To protect self-conscious students, you could fill in several blanks with fake values. Please indicate any made-up values when you return the sheets to me.

You could begin by giving the sheet to students who are willing participants. To help maintain anonymity, if so desired, tell students they may fill in any set of blanks on the page. If you have the time, I would appreciate your helping them give the required information and the format requested. Please return the completed sheets to me within a few days, if possible. If you wish, I will supply you with the results of the survey.

I wonder how many of the "meanest" kids in our school you have in your classes!

The Meanest Kids in School

Who are the meanest boys and girls in our school? That is, what are the average (arithmetic mean) height, weight, and age of boys and girls in the freshman, sophomore, junior, and senior classes? Your *voluntary* participation in this informal survey will help in making these determinations.

On the chart below, please provide your gender, grade, height in inches (for example, 5' 7" is [5 × 12] + 7, or 67 inches), weight in pounds, and age in months to the nearest month (for example, if you are 15, your age is [15 × 12] + the number of months since your last birthday).

Results of the survey—that is, the average height, weight, and age for boys and girls in each of the classes—will be posted. Perhaps you are the "meanest" person in your class! In any case, thank you for your participation.

Gender: M F   Grade_____   Ht._____   Wt._____   Age_____

Gender: M F   Grade_____   Ht._____   Wt._____   Age_____

Gender: M F   Grade_____   Ht._____   Wt._____   Age_____

Gender: M F   Grade_____   Ht._____   Wt._____   Age_____

Gender: M F   Grade_____   Ht._____   Wt._____   Age_____

Gender: M F   Grade_____   Ht._____   Wt._____   Age_____

Gender: M F   Grade_____   Ht._____   Wt _____   Age_____

Gender: M F   Grade_____   Ht._____   Wt._____   Age_____

Gender: M F   Grade_____   Ht._____   Wt._____   Age_____

Gender: M F   Grade_____   Ht._____   Wt._____   Age_____

Gender: M F   Grade_____   Ht._____   Wt._____   Age_____

Gender: M F   Grade_____   Ht._____   Wt._____   Age_____

Gender: M F   Grade_____   Ht._____   Wt._____   Age_____

Gender: M F   Grade_____   Ht._____   Wt._____   Age_____

Gender: M F   Grade_____   Ht._____   Wt._____   Age_____

Gender: M F   Grade_____   Ht._____   Wt _____   Age_____

Gender: M F   Grade_____   Ht._____   Wt._____   Age_____

Gender: M F   Grade_____   Ht._____   Wt._____   Age_____

Gender: M F   Grade_____   Ht._____   Wt._____   Age_____

Gender: M F   Grade_____   Ht._____   Wt._____   Age_____

Once the sheets are returned, allow the students to take over. They first need to discuss how the members of the class will analyze the information. Then the students should split up the data sheets and begin determining the mean, mode, and median height, weight, and age of the "average" boy and girl in the freshman, sophomore, junior, and senior classes.

After the statistics had been compiled, instruct the students to obtain some people-size paper, perhaps from the art department. Once this is done they can put it on the floor and then have the person in class whose height and weight are closest to that of the "average" person serve as a model. He or she is to lie down on the paper and have his or her outline traced. These profiles can be labeled and posted in the hallway for all to see.

As mentioned earlier, problems from the students' world are interesting and meaningful to students, and they enjoy doing them. There are not too many of these problems that fit into the typical curriculum, but you should try to incorporate a few of them into your lessons during the school year.

Chapter Seven

He Who Laughs, Lasts

Humor in the Classroom

This chapter contains suggestions and resources to help you to integrate humor into the classroom.

You probably know people who are naturally humorous. They have a very special gift of being able to make others laugh. Kids like to be entertained, and although it is not an educator's primary job, teachers who display a sense of humor seem more human to the students. A good sense of humor usually helps to improve the classroom atmosphere and the rapport between students and the teacher. Consequently, it makes classroom management easier. If you have a natural sense of humor, use it as an effective tool in the classroom.

What if you are not naturally funny? Can you still infuse humor into the classroom? Absolutely! Below are some suggestions for doing this.

MATH RIDDLES

Math riddles can be found by searching online. They can be used as a beginning- or end-of-class activity or inserted into the lesson any time you feel it would be effective to do so. Below are some examples.

1. What is the opposite of a stop sign?
2. Why is a meter stick a stubborn ruler?
3. What do magicians do between April 30 and June 1?
4. What do you call a parrot that should go on a diet?
5. How does a blind trigonometry teacher teach?

Answers: 1. A cosine; 2. It won't give an inch; 3. Matrix; 4. Polynomial ("Polly no meal"); 5. By using sine language.

Yes, they are corny, but the kids do seem to enjoy them.

HUMOROUS STORY PROBLEMS

Here is a humorous story that can be used when covering a unit on geometric sequences and series or any time you think it is appropriate. Give the students the following problem.

The Rabbit in the Box

A rabbit is inside a rectangular box that has holes in the front and back. The rabbit sticks its head out of the hole in the front; one minute later it sticks its head out of the hole in the back; one-half (1/2) minute later it sticks its head out of the hole in the front; a quarter (1/4) minute later, out of the hole in the back; an eighth (1/8) minute later out of the hole in the front; and so on. If the pattern continues, after how long will the rabbit be sticking its head out of both holes at the same time? The formula for the sum of an infinite geometric sequence is

$$S = a/(1-r).$$

Many students will grab their pencils and papers and begin to work on the problem. It won't be long before one student says something like, "Wait a minute! In reality the rabbit will never be sticking hits head out of both holes at the same time!" You can respond, "You're correct, of course, unless you want to split hares!"

Chances are the students will respond with some laughter, but you will likely hear moans and groans. However, many students will realize that you went through the trouble of writing and presenting the problem just to get in a poor pun. You will probably notice smiles on almost every face; many do appreciate the effort made, and the rapport between you and the class will probably improve.

A Question for the Ages

Nick is a 35-year-old math teacher while his daughter Alicia is 5. He is seven times as old as her. Five years pass. He is now 40 and she is 10. He is now four times as old as her. Five more years pass. Nick is now 45 while Alicia is 15. His age is three times hers. Fifteen years pass. He is now 60 and she is 30. Now he is twice as old as her.

Nick	Alicia	Multiplication Factor
35	5	7
40	10	4
45	15	3
60	30	2

Question: After how many more years will Nick and Alicia be the same age?

Some students will probably attempt to calculate the answer, but most should realize that Nick and Alicia will never be the same age. Students usually enjoy this problem, and while it is amusing, it can be used in an educational way. This story can be told at the beginning of a unit on ratios. It is a different introduction and typically gets the attention of the students and readies them for the lesson to come.

This story can also be used to introduce the concept of limits. You can probably think of other ways to use this story.

MATH JOKES

Many math jokes can be found online. They can be either of a general natural or geared to a specific topic.

The Mathematician and the Horse

There once was a mathematician who owned a very intelligent horse. He taught the horse arithmetic. He taught the horse algebra and geometry, but when he attempted to teach the horse Cartesian geometry, the coordinate geometry system invented by the seventeenth-century French mathematician René Descartes (pronounced *day cart*), the horse was unable to learn it. What is the moral of the story?

Answer: Don't put Descartes before the horse.

Most students groan when the punch line is given, but almost all of them enjoy the humorous aspect of the story.

"Wacky Definitions" is very popular with the students, especially those who are taking or have completed a course in geometry. A good time to use this activity is the day before a vacation.

WACKY DEFINITIONS

Directions: Match each definition with the word or phrase below that describes it. To get the correct answers, you need to take liberties with the pronunciations of some of the words.

1. What you do with a worm
2. The mother of Minnie
3. What you do in a court in heaven
4. Fred Nomial's sister
5. A man who has spent much time in the sun
6. If you don't tell the truth, then you're _____
7. What you do when it rains
8. What the acorn said after it grew up
9. The Little Mermaid wears one
10. When your parrot flies away
11. April Fool's prank one month late
12. An extremist
13. A miner's occupational hazard
14. What the square tree had
15. A tall coffee pot perking
16. Italian mass transit
17. Angles that say nice things to each other
18. What you get when you beat on a tree trunk
19. Where an escaped prisoner might hide
20. What you use to plow up a pro

a. polygon
b. polynomial
c. coefficient
d. tangent
e. line
f. radical
g. square roots
h. coincide
i. matrix
j. triangles
k. rhombus
l. minimum
m. complementary angles
n. algebra
o. protractor
p. hypotenuse

q. concave
r. geometry
s. collinear
t. logarithm

Answers: 1-c, 2-l, 3-j, 4-b, 5-d, 6-e, 7-h, 8-r, 9-n, 10-a, 11-i, 12-f, 13-s, 14-g, 15-p, 16-k, 17-m, 18-t, 19-q, 20-o

Chapter Eight

Calculate This!

Using the Graphing Calculator

Calculators, especially graphing calculators, play a prominent role in math education. This chapter provides strategies and activities for the use of the graphing calculator.

Those who were in high school in the 1960s had a calculator that was narrow, generally cylindrical in shape, made of wood, and about 7 inches long. One end contained graphite and was used for entering data while the other, rubbery end was used to delete entries. Yes, your calculator was a pencil. In those days, actual calculators were rare.

Today, calculators, especially graphing calculators, play a prominent role in math education. The danger, of course, is abusing them. Many students grab their calculator when faced with a problem like multiplying 4 × 6. This is a clear misuse of a graphing calculator. That's like using a sledge hammer to crack a walnut!

Unfortunately, that seems to be the way it is. Kids have grown up with calculators and use them for even the easiest problems. Students seem to enjoy using the calculator and often are motivated to do the math because of it. Several problems using the graphing calculator should be interjected into the curriculum throughout a math course.

Many textbooks contain graphing calculator activities. You may also be able to find such activities in support materials from the publisher of the students' text. In addition, there are several books, independent of any specific textbook, that are good sources of these problems. Check online.

It can be very time consuming to write problems for the graphing calculator. If you enjoy writing problems and have the time to do so (you should have plenty of time in July and August), perhaps you can seek out colleagues who share the same interest. A small network of problem writers can be organized and agree to share the problems they have written. If there were such of group of perhaps five people, and if they each wrote one problem per quarter, at the end of the year you would have (don't you dare use your calculator!) 20 problems. After a few years you would have access to a library of good problems.

Before doing an activity using the graphing calculators, take an informal survey in your classes to see how many students own their own. Check with your department chair to see if the department has graphing calculators and how to go about borrowing them for use in your classroom. Also ask about security measures you need to take to ensure all calculators are returned. With that information at hand, plan your lesson in advance.

Be aware that some students are probably very efficient with the graphing calculator, while others do not know how to take off the cover. When doing the lesson, it is probably a good idea to partner a student who is proficient with the graphing calculator with one who is not. Also be aware that the lesson you teach will probably take more time than you anticipate due to the inefficiency of some students with the calculator.

Below are a few examples of the type of problems that help show the problem-solving capabilities of the graphing calculator. (Please note that the instructions for each of the problems are written for the TI-83/TI-83+ or the TI-84/TI-84+. If a different calculator is used, adjustments may have to be made.)

The following is a classic problem which can be used from lower-level classes through more advanced courses.

THE OPEN BOX

You have a square piece of metal, 18 inches by 18 inches. From this square you wish to make an open box by cutting square corners from the metal and then folding up the sides. How long should the side of the cutout square be in order for the box to have *maximum* volume?

If some students seem to have trouble understanding the concept, pass out blank paper, a ruler, and scissors to each student. Have them measure an 18-by-18 square (or some other convenient size) and cut out four congruent corners and fold them up to form an open box. As an alternative approach, you can do the demonstration. Once this is done, students are ready to work on the solution.

Length of Side of Cutout Square (don't forget units)	Dimensions of the Open Box's Base	Volume (in cubic units)

Figure 8.1

As mentioned above, this problem has the flexibility to be solved at several levels.

Solution by Arithmetic

Here a graphing calculator is not necessary. Students simply fill in the left-hand column of Figure 8.1 with the integers from 1 to 9. They next fill in the possible dimensions of the box in the middle column. Doing the cutting and folding, or watching you do the demonstration, usually helps the students with this part. It is also advisable that students draw and carefully label a diagram. They can then use a calculator to fill in column three. Finally, by inspection of the data, they can see that cutting out a square 3 inches by 3 inches will result in the maximum volume.

Note that only integral values were considered in column one. However, if it is a lower-level math class, this solution is usually sufficient.

Solution Using the Graphing Calculator and Lists

(Note: Depending upon the students' skill level with the calculator, they should help you to navigate through these steps, or perhaps they can do some or all of it on their own or with a partner or group.)

- Go to [STAT], then Edit and hit [ENTER].
- Move the cursor up so that it highlights L1.
- Next go to [LIST], then hit [OPS], seq, [ENTER].
- L1 = seq (should appear at the bottom of the display.
- Set L1 = seq (x,x,1,9,1) and hit [ENTER]. This fills in column one with the integers from 1 through 9.

- Now move the cursor to the right and up to highlight L_2.
- At the bottom of the display set L2 = $(18 - 2L1)^2$. Hit [ENTER] This lists the areas of the bases for the values in column one.
- Now move the cursor to the right and up to highlight L_3.
- Set L3 = L1*L2. Hit [ENTER]. Column three will now be filled in with the volumes corresponding to the data displayed in L1 and L2. The solution is determined by inspection.

Again, we have only used integral values in L_1. How can we be sure that the maximum value does not occur for a value of x that is not an integer? The next two solutions deal with this concern.

Solution Using the Graphing Calculator and a Graph

By drawing a diagram and calling the side of the cut-out square x, students should be able to determine that the dimensions of the box are $x(18 - 2x)^2$. Students can discover this on their own, with a partner, or in their groups, or you can lead the class to make this discovery. In any case, the volume equals
$$V(x) = x(18 - 2x)^2 \text{ or } 4x^3 - 72x^2 + 324x$$
Enter this expression in the y= menu. Instruct the students to determine a suitable window. Some are very good at this while others need help. The following settings work well:

- x min 0, y min 0
- x max 10, y max 500
- x scl 1, y scl 50

Once the function is entered and the window is set, hit [GRAPH]. The graph should be displayed on the screen. Now use [TRACE] to *estimate* the maximum value. Or, hit [2nd] [TRACE] maximum. Move the cursor to the left of the vertex; hit [ENTER]. Move the cursor to the right of the vertex; hit [ENTER] [ENTER]. The maximun value can now be read off the screen.

Solution Using Calculus

Again, students must determine that $V(x) = 4x^3 - 72x^2 + 324x$.

To find the value of x that produces the maximum value of $V(x)$, find $V'(x)$ and set it equal to zero; that is, $V'(x) = 12x^2 - 144x + 324 = 0$. This equation can now be solved by factoring, completing the square, using the quadratic formula, or drawing its graph on the graphing calculator and finding the x intercepts. Once x is determined, calculating $V(x)$ results in the solution.

The next problem shows an application of the Pythagorean theorem.

THE SHORTEST PATH PROBLEM

Graphing Calculator Activity

Below is a diagram made by the water company. They want to connect two new houses, H1 and H2, to their main water line. To keep down the cost, they want to use the least amount of pipe possible. If the distance from H1 to A is 800 feet, the distance from H2 to B is 600 feet, and the distance from A to B is 1500 feet, where on the main water line AB should point X be located?

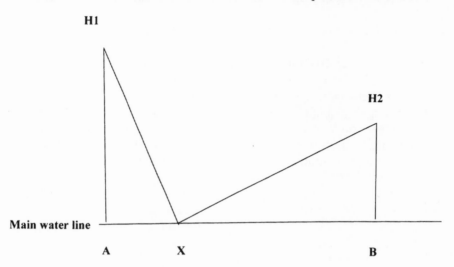

The Shortest Path Problem—Solution

- Begin by clearing the lists: hit [STAT]; clear list (enter the list[s] you want cleared, separated by commas; for example, L1, L3, L6) OR
- Hit [STAT], then edit, then hit [ENTER]; move cursor over "Ln" at the top of the list and hit [CLEAR].
- Hitting [2nd] [MODE] takes you back to the home screen.
- L1 = AX, which varies from 0 to 1500.
- Hit [STAT], edit, hit [ENTER], and move the cursor on top of "L1"; then go to LIST, OPS, seq; hit [ENTER].
- Set Seq (variable, variable, start, end, increment); in this case seq (x,x,0,1500,100); hit [ENTER]. L1 should now be filled in.
- L2 = H_1X = the square root of $(800^2 + AX^2)$ = the square root of $(800^2 + L1^2)$; move cursor on top of "L2"; hit [ENTER].
- At the bottom of the screen write L2 = the square root of $(800^2 + L1^2)$ and hit [ENTER]; L2 should be filled in.

- L3 = XB = 1500 − AX = 1500 − L1; move the cursor on top of "L3"; hit [ENTER].
- At the bottom of the screen write L3 =1500 − L1; hit [ENTER]. L3 should be filled in.
- L4 = H_2X = the square root of $(600^2 + L3^2)$; move the cursor on top of "L4"; hit [ENTER].
- At bottom of screen write L4 = the square root of $(600^2 + L3^2)$; hit [ENTER]. L4 should be filled in.
- L5 = H_1X + H_2X = L2 + L4; move the cursor on top of "L5" and hit [ENTER].
- At bottom of screen write L5 = L2 + L4; hit [ENTER]. L5 should be filled in.
- Scroll the cursor down the values in L5 and stop on the minimum, in the case 2052.7. Then scroll left to find the value in L1 that corresponds to this minimum value in L5, in this case 900.
- Examining the list in L5 more closely, it cannot be concluded with certainty that the minimum value is 2052.7, but it should be clear that the minimum value is somewhere between 2053.3 and 2061.6. Therefore to get a more accurate minimum value, values in L1 between 800 and 1000 need to be considered. To do this, the lists need to be changed.
- Go back to L1 and move the cursor on top of "L1." Hit [CLEAR]; the list remains (for now), and the cursor should be at the bottom of the screen.
- Go to List, OPS, seq; then enter seq(x,x,800,1000,10) and hit [ENTER]. A new list of values should appear in L1.
- Lists L2 through L5 must now be changed.
- Place the cursor on top of "L2" and hit [CLEAR]. At the bottom of the screen, enter the appropriate expression for L2 (see above).
- Follow the same procedure for L3 through L5.
- Scroll down L5 to find the minimum value, in this case 2051.8; then scroll left to find the value in L1 that corresponds with the minimum value in L5, in this case 860.

Is it practical to "fine tune" the data further?

Note to the teacher: In the problem "Bones, Bones, Bones!" as an alternative to filling in just the table, the day before you do this activity ask all the students to come to class the next day prepared to give you their heights and the lengths of their tibia bones. You can then list the data on the board and enter all the ordered pairs into the calculator.

BONES, BONES, BONES!

A person's *tibia* bone is the inner and larger of the two bones in the lower leg. It extends from the ankle to the knee. A relationship exists between the length of a person's tibia and the person's height. In this activity you will determine that relationship and use it to play detective. Using a tape measure, carefully measure the length of several classmates' tibias and heights in centimeters. (Note: There are 2.54 cm per inch). Enter the data in the table below.

x-Tibia (cm.)									
y-Height (cm.)									

Figure 8.3

Using the entries in the chart, find the equation of the line representing this data and draw its graph using the graphing calculator. Here's how to do it:

- Begin by going to [STAT]; then edit, then [ENTER].
- Clear any data that is currently in the table by moving the cursor onto L1, then press [CLEAR], then [ENTER]. Then move your cursor to L2 and press [CLEAR], then [ENTER.]
- Enter the *x* values (tibia) from Figure 8.3 into L1 and the *y* values (height) into L2. After each entry hit [ENTER].
- Pressing [2nd] [MODE] takes you back to the home screen.
- Clear the y= menu by hitting [Y=], then [CLEAR].
- Look at the data in the table. Adjust the window by hitting [WINDOW] and choosing appropriate values of Xmin, Xmax, Xscl, Ymin, Ymax, and Yscl.

To get a scatter plot,

- Press [2nd] [Y=] [1], go to ON, and press [ENTER].
- For type, go to the first chart—that is, the scatter plot—and hit [ENTER].
- Make sure the X list states L1 and the Y list states L2.
- Go to Mark and choose the symbol you want to show on the scatter plot and hit [ENTER].
- Now hit [GRAPH]. The scatter plot should appear on the screen.

When you get your plot, does it look like you expected? Is all your information there? If not, go to [WINDOW] and make any necessary adjustments.
To find the equation of the line of best fit:

- Hit [STAT], then move to CALC. Bring the cursor down to the appropriate regression (in this case it is LinReg) and press [ENTER].
- On your screen you should have LinReg. Now press [2nd] [1] [,] [2nd] [2] [,] and [VARS]; move to Y-VARS. 1:Function should be on your screen. Hit [ENTER] three times.
- [Y=] will give you the equation of the line of best fit. Record it below:

- [GRAPH] will graph the line, which should now appear on the screen.

CSI Case

Over a 30-year period, five hikers have been reported missing in the Sleeping Giant State Park in Hamden, Connecticut. One day a man was hiking with his dog, which dug up a bone in the general area where the five hikers had disappeared. Lab tests indicated that the bone was a human tibia; its length was 45.1 cm. Based on the relationship you discovered above (the equation of the line of best fit) and the heights of the missing hikers, determine whose bone was likely discovered.

Name	*Height*
Boots, Bernie	198 cm
Camper, Chris	170 cm
Tent, Thomas	152 cm
Trail, Terry	185 cm
Walker, Wilber	161 cm

In this chapter you have seen some strategies and activities for using the graphing calculator. Try to incorporate several lessons like these throughout the school year. The students enjoy them and can learn a lot of math in the process.

Chapter Nine

The Pen Is Mightier
Than the Calculator

Writing and Reading in a Math Class

Students study a lot of math while they are in school. After graduation, however, the amount of math the average person uses decreases significantly, while reading and writing are skills people use for the rest of their lives. This chapter contains suggestions and activities to improve the students' reading and writing skills in a math class.

ANSWER COMPLETELY

There are many opportunities when you are quizzing or testing your students, or calling on them in class, to require them to provide an answer in a complete sentence using appropriate mathematical vocabulary. For example, instead of accepting "359" as the answer to a word problem in geometry, require the student to give an answer such as, "Because the diameter of the pool is 24 feet, the surface area of the liner is 754 square feet. Therefore it will cost Chris $359 to replace the lining on his pool."

READ CAREFULLY

When you give students quizzes, tests, or handouts such as activities or projects, encourage them to underline, circle, or highlight key directions, concepts, important data, and so forth. During the first few weeks of a course, when you hand out materials, go through this procedure with them.

After a while, most will catch on to the process and your help will no longer be needed.

WRITE RAPIDLY

When students first enter the room, pass out paper and ask them to write the questions and concerns they have had since the last time the class met. You can skim the papers quickly (perhaps while the students are doing the opening-of-class activity) and respond to the students sometime before the class ends.

FROM TOP TO BOTTOM

This is a writing activity that helps students review material; it is especially helpful to do this the day before a test.

1. On a piece of paper, instruct the students to draw a horizontal line about midway between the top and bottom.
2. Write a comment or question on the board such as, "What are the properties of a rhombus?" Or, list all the laws of exponents that you know.

- Give students an appropriate amount of time to respond to the prompt. Tell them to write their answers on the top half of the paper.
- Ask several students to go to the board and write their responses; eliminate duplicate answers.
- Ask those students sitting at their seats to put check marks next to those responses on their papers that match what is written on the board.
- Tell students to write the answers from the board that they don't have on the top half of their paper on the bottom half.

CHALK TALK

This is a classic activity that can be used from middle school through college. "Chalk Talk" is a silent form of communication between students and the teacher and between students and students. It provides an excellent change of pace for all and is usually a very worthwhile and enjoyable activity. Chalk Talk can be done for a few minutes or the entire period.

- To begin, explain very briefly that this is a *silent* activity—no talking is allowed. Anyone who wishes may respond, in writing, to the prompt written at the chalk board, or white board, or on large sheets of paper taped to the walls.

- Write a prompt, in the form of a question or statement, on the board; for example,

    What is most difficult about the material in this chapter?

    How is the topic we are studying used in the real world?

    The thing I like most about what we are doing now is…

    The thing I like least about what we are doing now is…

    To prepare for the test on this material I will…

    I feel I would be better prepared for this test if the teacher would re-explain…

- Make chalk (or markers) available to everyone, or place chalk (or markers) at the board.
- Those who wish may respond in writing to the prompt, or they may respond to the comments or questions made by other students.
- You may respond to a response with a comment or a question or sit back and do nothing.
- You decide when to end the session.

The first time you use Chalk Talk it may not run smoothly. But as with most activities, the more you do it, the more efficient you will become at facilitating it. Every Chalk Talk session is different; don't be afraid to try it.

For more detailed information on Chalk Talk and for further examples of possible prompts to use, go online and search for "chalk talk."

In this chapter you have been given a number of suggestions and activities to improve the students' reading and writing skills in a math class. Try to incorporate several in your lessons during the school year.

Chapter Ten

It's Game Time

Classroom Competitions

This chapter presents a variety of classroom-tested competitions and games that you can use to enhance learning and have fun.

OVERVIEW

Playing games in the classroom can

- help the students to learn the course content.
- make drill and practice pleasant and successful.
- offer a change of pace for both the students and the teacher.
- be useful in providing for individual differences.
- motivate students to improve study habits.
- cultivate more desirable attitudes toward mathematics.
- relate mathematical topics to individual interests.
- be used to introduce new mathematical ideas.
- give more students a chance to be successful.
- encourage cooperation among students.
- help promote student leadership.
- be a lot of fun for both the students and the teacher.

The results of a student survey pertaining to classroom competitions (see next section) seem to indicate that the students derive many benefits from classroom competitions.

Chapter 10

STUDENT SURVEY

(A summary of 223 responses is provided for each item.)

Course _____ Period _____ Date _____

I am interested in your opinion regarding classroom competitions. Below are several statements. Please respond to each by indicating the degree with which you agree or disagree with the statement. Use the following code:

SA means you *S*trongly *A*gree

MA means you *M*ostly *A*gree

MD means you *M*ostly *D*isagree

SD means you *S*trongly *D*isagree

Circle your choice. Use the space below each item for comments.

The various classroom competitions have . . .

1. helped to improve my math skills.

SA	MA	MD	SD
35%	57%	7%	1%
92%		8%	

2. improved my attitude towards math.

SA	MA	MD	SD
22%	59%	17%	2%
81%		19%	

3. motivated me to improve my study skills.

SA	MA	MD	SD
15%	55%	24%	5%
70%		29%	

4. improved my ability to cooperate with others.

SA	MA	MD	SD
30%	57%	10%	3%
87%		13%	

The games below have been classroom tested over several years.

TIC-TAC-TOE

This game can be used for drill and practice or to go over homework. It doesn't take prior preparation and can be done virtually any time in the class period. Whenever you feel that the class is dragging and you want to raise the energy level, consider playing this game.

To begin, put the traditional tic-tac-toe lines on the board. For easier reference, number the cells.

1	2	3
4	5	6
7	8	9

Let's say you are going to use this game for extra practice on a simple topic, such as using the laws of exponents. Say something like "Students, turn to page 127. We are going to play a team game using problems 1 through 20. The teams will be the left half of the room, which is the X team, against the right half, which is the O team. I will give you all a problem to do; after a few seconds I will call on someone. If that person gets the correct answer, he or she will tell me into which cell the team letter (X or O) will be placed. If the person is incorrect, I will call on someone from the other team. If he or she is correct then he or she can indicate into which cell the team letter will be placed. The first team to get the traditional three in a row wins the game."

MOTION GAMES IN THE CLASSROOM

These games are primarily used for drill and practice. They add an element of motion, which the students seem to enjoy.

Station to Station

On 5" × 7" index cards (or half sheets of paper), write the problems to be solved, one per card. Number the cards and place one on each desk in the room. Give each student a piece of paper on which to copy the problem and write the solution. Also provide an answer sheet numbered from 1 to as many problems as you are using.

Tell the students that at your signal they are to copy the problem in front of them onto the paper provided, solve it, and put the answer in the appropriate place on the answer sheet. After you say "begin," each student works on the problem. After a sufficient amount of time, instruct students to *change stations*; that is, to move to another desk according to a plan students were given prior to the beginning of the game. (It's probably a good idea to display a diagram of the plan on the board.) While at the new desk, again students are to copy the problem, work it out, and put the answer on the answer sheet in the right place. This process continues until each student has done every problem. At that point, go over the answers and address any problems that caused trouble for the students. This game works especially well with younger students, but older students seem to enjoy it also.

Logjam

This game is similar to Station to Station. Again have problems for the students to work on written on 5" × 7" file cards, one at each desk. However, this time, after the student has finished the problem, he or she immediately passes it on to another student according to a plan explained to them prior to the game. (Again, it is probably a good idea to display a diagram of the plan on the board.) As might be expected, the slower-working students do not pass on the problems as quickly as most, hence the name "Logjam."

It is wise to have some extra problems, perhaps of a more challenging nature, on the board for those who have a long wait between problems.

After all the students have done all the problems, go over the answers and provide help with those problems that caused trouble.

WHO AM I?

This game was conceived as a team activity, but it can be played on an individual basis.

- To begin, the students move into their regular cooperative learning groups. (If groups are not regularly used, they can be put together for the purposes of this game.)
- Make a transparency of the clues (see the following section for samples). Put the transparency on the overhead projector, but mask all but the first clue. (If an overhead projector is not available, the clues could be written on the board). The objective is for the team to guess the solution using a minimum number of clues.
- If a team thinks they have the solution, they say "stop." Then they write the question number and the answer on a small piece of paper, along with their team name, and bring the paper to you. If the team is correct, the point value of the clue is awarded and the round is over. If the team is not correct, they score *zero* and the team is eliminated from this round of play. The game continues; that is, additional clues are revealed, one at a time, until the last clue is given.
- At any point a team may guess the answer (following the procedure given above) in an attempt to gain the point value of the clue. Obviously, seeing more clues increases their chance of getting the correct answer, but it also lowers the potential score. (Decisions, decisions!)
- After the final clue is revealed, the scores for round one are recorded. The running scores should be listed on the board, and the game continues.
- At the end of the game the winning team(s) or individuals are rewarded with extra credit, candy, or other prizes.

Below are some sample clues that can be used for this game.

Sample Clues for "Who Am I?"

Points

1.	5	I am a two-digit number; call me x.
	4	I am larger than 30 but smaller than 85; that is, $30 < x < 85$.
	3	I am a perfect square.
	2	The sum of my digits is 9.
	1	I am the solution of the equation $2x + 3 = 75$.
		(Solution: I am 36.)

2.   5   I am an eight-letter word.

      4   I contain two *e*'s and one *o*.

      3   I have a powerful personality.

      2   I am a superscript.

      1   When I am a positive integer, I tell how many times a base
             is used as a factor.

             (Solution: I am an exponent.)

3.   5   I am a two-digit number; call me *z*.

      4   I am larger than 0 but smaller than 70; that is, $0 < z < 70$.

      3   One of my digits is a 6.

      2   I am a perfect square.

      1   I am also a perfect cube.

             (Solution: I am 64.)

4.   5   I am a two-digit number; call me *x*.

      4   My square is between 130 and 300; that is, $130 < x^2 < 300$

      3   My units digit is prime.

      2   The sum of my digits is less than 8.

      1   Those who fear me have triskaidekaphobia.

             (Solution: I am 13.)

5.   5   I am a one-digit number; call me *x*.

      4   I am a solution to one of the following equations: $x^2 = 1$, $x^2 = 4$, $x^2 = 9$.

      3   I am not positive.

      2   My absolute value is greater than 1; that is, $|x| > 1$.

      1   My square is an odd number.

             (Solution: I am – 3.)

6.   5   I am a one-digit number; call me *v*.

      4   I am larger than –4 but smaller than 4; that is, $-4 < v < 4$.

      3   I am not negative.

      2   I am the square of myself.

      1   I am not positive.

             (Solution: I am 0.)

7.   5   I am an eight-letter word.

       4   I have a balanced personality.

       3   I begin with an *e* and end with an *n*.

       2   I contain a *t* and a *q*.

       1   I am a statement that two quantities are equal.

          (Solution: I am an equation.)

8.   5   I am a two-digit number; call me *x*.

       4   I am less than the number of different outcomes when a card is drawn from a deck.

       3   I am more than 3 times the highest possible sum when two regular dice are rolled.

       2   Both my digits are odd.

       1   Both my digits are prime.

          (Solution: I am 37.)

9.   5   I am a one-digit number.

       4   I am greater than *x* when $5x - 3 = 17$.

       3   I am less than *y* when $-4y + 8 = -28$.

       2   I am odd.

       1   I am associated with Snow White.

          (Solution: I am 7.)

10.   5   I am a three-digit number.

       4   All my digits are the same.

       3   All my digits are odd

       2   All my digits are prime.

       1   The sum of my digits is a perfect square.

          (Solution: I am 333.)

WHAT AM I?

This game lends itself very nicely to geometry classes when reviewing definitions or properties of figures. The rules are the same as those for "Who Am I?"

Sample Clues for "What Am I?"

Points

1. 5   I am a geometric figure.

    4   I have no width, but I have length.

    3   My length is infinite.

    2   I have an endpoint.

    1   I am associated with the sun.

    (Solution: I am a ray.)

2. 5   I am an instrument used to make measurements.

    4   Part of me is a straight edge.

    3   Part of me is curved.

    2   I am used to measure angles.

    1   When voting on tractors, I vote pro.

    (Solution: I am a protractor.)

3. 5   I am a geometric figure.

    4   I am not a quadrilateral.

    3   I have an even number of sides.

    2   The number of sides I have is a perfect cube.

    1   Stop signs are made in my shape.

    (Solution: I am an octagon.)

4. 5   I am associated with polygons.

    4   I am a type of angle.

    3   I'm on the outside looking in.

    2   I always extend myself.

    1   I am adjacent to an interior angle.

    (Solution: I am an exterior angle.)

5. 5   I am a geometric term of two words.

    4   I can be a segment, line, ray, or plane.

    3   I pass through a segment.

    2   Some say I have a split personality.

    1   I intersect a segment at its midpoint.

    (Solution: I am a segment bisector.)

6. 5   I am a line segment.

    4   I can be found in a triangle.

    3   When in a triangle, there are three of me.

    2   I extend from a vertex to the line containing the opposite side.

    1   I form a right angle.

    (Solution: I am an altitude.)

7. 5   I am a polygon.

    4   My name contains two words.

    3   I am formed by three noncollinear segments.

    2   Some think I am sharp.

    1   All my angles are less than 90 degrees.

    (Solution: I am an acute triangle.)

8. 5   I am a line segment.

    4   Every triangle has three of me.

    3   I extend from a vertex to the opposite side.

    2   I bisect the opposite side.

    1   My name is sometimes associated with a strip of land down the center of a highway.

    (Solution: I am a median.)

THE MESSAGE GAME

This game is typically played to go over homework, although it can be used for drill and practice. This is a team game with the winning team earning a reward such as candy or extra credit.

1. To begin, the students move into their regular cooperative learning groups. (If groups are not regularly used, they can be put together for the purposes of this game.)
2. If the task is to go over homework, give the students a few minutes with their teammates to discuss the previous assignment in an attempt to reach consensus on the answers. While they are doing this, put blank spaces on the board (or overhead projector) that when filled in will form a short sentence or message. Some suggestions are given below.

3. List on the board all the team names in random order.

4. After each team has indicated that they are ready to go, the game begins. The object of the game is to guess what the message is. (This game is similar to "Hangman.")

5. To start, call on the team at the top of the list. Choose a problem, and the team spokesperson (usually the taskmaster) gives the answer. If the answer is correct, that team chooses a letter (consonant or vowel) in an attempt to fill in one or more of the blank spaces. If the letter is part of one or more of the words, it is put into the blank space(s).

6. After a team gives a correct answer to the math problem and selects a letter that is in the message, they may guess what the sentence says; there is no penalty for a wrong guess. If they are correct, they have won the game; if not, the turn passes to the next team on the list. If a team gives a wrong answer, the same question is given to the next team on the list. Neither the question nor the incorrect answer is repeated; it is each team's responsibility to pay attention to what is going on!

7. Continue down the list of team names, calling on each team until a correct answer is given. Again the team chooses a letter and, if correct, may try to guess the message. If they are not successful, go back to the list and pick the next team in order that has not had a first attempt at a problem.

8. The procedure is continued until the message is guessed.

Sometimes you may run out of homework questions before the game is completed. Consequently, it is wise to have some extra problems ready, perhaps from supplementary questions in the back of the book, from a chapter review, worksheet, or other source. Also, if time is running out and it is obvious that the game cannot be completed using the stated rules, simply fill in letters in the blank spaces one at a time, and the first team to correctly state the message wins.

Some suggested messages include the following:

- Winners make commitments.
- If you believe it, you can achieve it.
- Quitters never win; winners never quit.
- To break a bad habit, drop it.
- We trip over pebbles, not mountains.
- Discipline yourself so others won't have to.
- Excuses are for losers.
- By failing to prepare, you are preparing to fail.
- Make an effort, not an excuse.
- Quitting is not an option.

- There is no excuse for abuse.
- Be yourself. Everyone else is taken.

After the message is completed, it is interesting to ask the students what it means. This is one of the few opportunities to discuss in a math class some of the issues raised by the above statements.

On the lighter side, try these messages:

- If you don't pay your exorcist, you get repossessed.
- When a clock is hungry, it goes back for seconds.
- Every calendar's days are numbered.
- A boiled egg in the morning is hard to beat.
- Once you've seen one shopping center, you've seen a mall.
- Acupuncture is a jab well done.
- Santa's helpers are subordinate clauses.
- Reading while sunbathing will make you well red.
- When two egotists meet, it's an I for an I.
- A backward poet writes inverse.

TEAM TOURNAMENT

The "Team Tournament" is a favorite of students. At times they will ask to play this game. Initially it requires some work to get the materials ready, but once they are prepared you have most of them to use many times during a year or career.

Overview

Students are divided into heterogeneous cooperative learning teams to prepare for a tournament. During the intergroup competition, the students individually compete against members of about the same ability level from other teams. The teams whose members do the best in competition earn some type of reward (extra credit, candy, pens, etc.).

Materials Needed

Each student will need a problem sheet, a challenge sheet, and appropriate tools (pencil, calculator, etc.).

Each competitive group will need a pack of number squares (preferably color coded for easier sorting) consisting of numbers representing each problem to be done, two "double-point-value" squares, and one "triple-point-value" square; one scorecard; one answer sheet; and scrap paper.

Procedures

- After you have covered the material, assign students to learning teams of three to five members. (If cooperative learning groups are normally used, assigning new learning teams is unnecessary.)
- Give them study questions or problems similar to those that will be used during the competition. Teammates study together, attempting to prepare each member for competition, because the chances of winning are greatly increased if all team members are well prepared.
- The team tournament is usually held the next day.

The Tournament

- Assign team members to a group to compete against members of about the same ability level from the other teams. Use previous grades and your personal judgment to construct the competitive groups.
- Group members determine who takes the roles of scorer and timekeeper.
- Give each player a sheet of questions and a challenge sheet.
- Give each group a set of number squares (see "Materials Needed"), a scorecard, an answer sheet, and scrap paper.
- Instruct each group to spread out the number squares face down on the desk. Each player draws a number, the highest going first. Once that is decided, the player to the right of this person is given the answer sheet, which should be placed face down. Play rotates clockwise.
- When it is his or her turn, the player draws a number square, which indicates the problem to be done on the question sheet. Each problem is worth one point. If a double- or triple-score square is drawn, the value of the problem is either two or three points, respectively, and the player draws again. All players attempt this problem.
- Before the time limit is reached, usually 30 to 60 seconds, the player must give an answer. The scorer asks if there are any challenges. All players wishing to challenge (including the scorer and person with the answer sheet) must write what they feel is the correct answer on the challenge sheet. All challenges are then shown simultaneously. The person with the answer sheet then looks up the correct answer.
- If the player who originally did the problem is correct, he or she scores 1 point (more if a double- or triple-point-value square has been previously drawn). If he or she is incorrect, the score is 0. If a player is unable to do a problem or is unable to answer within the time limit, his or her score is 0, and the challenge procedure is then in effect. All correct challenges earn the point value of that question, while all incorrect challenges lose the point value.

- After the scorekeeper records the scores for that round, play (and the answer sheet) rotate clockwise.
- Play continues until a predetermined time or number of rounds is reached.
- Once the game is over, the scorekeeper fills in the "Points Earned" column on the scorecard and returns it to you. Your task is to determine tournament points for each team as follows:
- If two students from the same team are in the same competitive group, their points earned are averaged and they count as one person.
- If there are n people in a group, the person finishing with the highest number of points earned is awarded n tournament points for his or her team. The second highest number of earned points is awarded $n - 1$ tournament points for his or her team, and so forth.
- You then add up the total number of tournament points earned by each team to determine the final standings. If the original teams do not have the same number of players in competition, the tournament points earned are averaged to determine the final standings.

In the Appendix are copies of blank challenge sheets and scorecards and a number array. These can be reproduced and used to play. For durability, the numbers could be reproduced on oak tag or some other heavy-duty paper. Also, there is a sample score sheet that should help explain the scoring process.

You and your students may struggle with this game the first time you play it; that is not uncommon. The next time you play it, begin by reviewing the rules and ask if the students have any questions. Having gone through it once, the students have a much better understanding of the rules and the flow of the game and usually have little or no trouble. The more they play it, the more smoothly it runs.

After you have played a game in class, ask the students for their input. Do this at the end of that class or at the beginning of the next one. Their thoughts on what they derived from the game, the strengths and weaknesses of the game, and any suggestions they have for improvement are often very helpful. Even if the students have no suggestions, they appreciate being asked their opinions.

As you can see by the results of the survey shown at the beginning of this chapter, games enhance learning and help improve the students' collaborative and study skills. They are also fun and offer a change of pace for you and your students.

Chapter Eleven

All Good Things Must Come to an End

Closing Activities

Properly closing the class helps students to understand the purpose of the lesson and how it will connect to future learning. This chapter presents several ways to close a class.

- You can say to your students something such as, "Suppose one of your classmates were absent today and he or she called, e-mailed, or texted you at home to find out what we did in class. I will give everyone 30 seconds to think about how you would respond to that person, and then I will call on someone to share his or her thoughts with us."
- Have each student write out the response to the above activity.
- Pass out a piece of lined paper and have the students complete the following statements:

  Today I didn't understand . . .

  The most important thing I learned today was . . .

  You can then have one or more students read their responses. Collect all the papers so you can read them and get an overview of what went on in class from the students' perspective.
- Use a prepared "Exit Slip." See the sample in the Appendix.
- About five minutes before the class ends, give the students a quick one- or two-question quiz that covers the main concepts presented. Mentioning the possibility of this happening at the beginning of class often motivates the students to pay closer attention to the lesson. To encourage note taking, you could allow students to use their notes while taking the quiz.
- Students could write up a short quiz that they feel covers the main ideas presented in the lesson. They can then exchange their quiz with a class-

mate. Each student then works out the problems. The finished work can then be returned to the writer, who corrects it and discusses the results with the person who took it.

- Some teachers require students to keep a mathematics journal. If you do, then a summary of what went on in class would make a good entry into the journal.

Chapter Twelve

But Wait . . . There's More!

Included in this chapter are some strategies or ideas not previously mentioned that have been successfully used in the classroom.

WAIT TIME

Consider the following approach used by the teacher in a typical classroom.

Teacher: Mike, in the graph of the equation $y = 2x + 6$, what is the slope of the line?

This teacher made a common mistake that happens every day in the classroom. The teacher ignored wait time. What's that? It is the time the teacher should *wait* before calling on a student for an answer. But why should the teacher use wait time?

In the classes of teachers who use wait time, the following can usually be observed:

- The student responses are longer.
- The responses are usually more appropriate.
- There are fewer students who fail to respond.
- The students seem to have more confidence when giving their answers.
- More high-level questions are asked.

In classes where teachers do not use wait time, few if any of these are observed. Based on these observations, it could be argued that sometimes silence is an effective teaching strategy.

Let's get back to Mike. The teacher began the question by using Mike's name. Now, Mike is the only student who is expected to respond; all the other students are "off the hook," and many of them are probably not even thinking about the answer. Contrast that to the following:

Teacher: In the graph of the equation $y = 2x + 6$, what is the slope of the line? [Wait about 5 to 10 seconds.] Mike, what is the answer?

See the difference? In this case the wait time allows many students time to prepare an answer because no one knows whom the teacher is going to call on.

Also, consider the following approach:

Teacher: Class, I have a question for you. I will ask it, wait 30 seconds, and then call on someone for the answer. In the graph of the equation $y = 2x + 6$, what is the slope of the line?

Now virtually everyone in the class is likely thinking about the question and the answer. The teacher waits 30 seconds and then calls on someone.

Wait time is an important classroom tool. Students need some time to think about the question and form an intelligent answer. There are far too many teachers who don't use wait time, and consequently their questioning techniques are often ineffective.

Using wait time allows more students to be actively involved in the lesson, which enhances the teacher's classroom management skills.

THE CONSULTANT

The following idea is a simple but powerful strategy used while students are working in groups. The students are exposed to an aspect of problem solving that is often encountered in the real world.

Begin by having students move into their cooperative learning groups. (If you don't regularly use groups, you can create them for this activity.) Now give the students a relatively sophisticated problem and tell them that the problem will count as a group quiz and each team member will get the same grade.

Before the students begin collaboration on the problem, tell them that one solution is to be handed in from each group. Students are to sign the bottom of the paper indicating their agreement with the solution. Also tell the students that you are available to help them with the problem; however, they are to consider you as a consultant. This means they can "hire" you to answer questions or to give them hints. However, as a company would have to do in the business world, they will have to "pay" you for the information. The payment is in terms of points, which are subtracted from their final score.

Some questions, for example those of a clarifying nature, are free of charge, but for the answers to significant questions you charge one point. Each major hint costs them two points.

Below is an example of a problem given to students in a geometry class, a problem that actually had to be dealt with in real life. For this particular problem the students were shown a copy of the letter sent by the water company. The authenticity of the problem makes the activity more meaningful to the students.

Water Consumption

Last summer Mr. Poole received a letter from the water company stating that the most recent reading of his water meter showed a significant increase in consumption compared to the same period during the previous year. To be more specific, the prior usage was 3,200 cubic feet of water compared to the more recent usage of 7,700 cubic feet. The water company wanted to know if Mr. Poole had an explanation for the increased water consumption; they feared there could be a leak in the fixtures or plumbing, which could waste hundreds of gallons of water.

Mr. Poole thought about the problem and the possible causes of the increased water consumption. He recalled that earlier that spring he had discovered a hole, caused by corrosion, in the side of his above-ground swimming pool, close to the bottom. The hole resulted in a slow leak. To repair the hole, approximately 90 percent of the pool water had to be removed. When the repairs were completed, the pool was refilled with water to a depth of 4.5 feet. If the diameter of the pool is 24 feet, could this refilling of the pool account for the increased water consumption described in the letter? Clearly support your answer using mathematics.

What usually happens is that most teams work hard on the problem; they don't want to pay you. If a group asks for help, you can walk over to them and answer their question using a soft enough voice so that only that group can hear you. Sometimes you can write out a response. You should have small slips of paper prepared, each containing one hint, to help groups who don't have specific questions but are having trouble finding the solution. They buy the slip containing the information and are provided no further help unless they wish to buy more hints.

The hints below can be cut into individual slips and sold to groups who request consultation.

- *Hint 1*—(cost 2 points): Begin by finding the volume of the filled pool ($V = \pi r^2 h$; in this case $h = 4.5$ feet).
- *Hint 2*—(cost 2 points): Find 90 percent of the volume of the filled pool.

- *Hint 3*—(cost 2 points): Find the difference in cubic feet of water used during the two years in question.

As the end of the time limit approaches, the student are reminded that your services as a consultant are still available. Now it is decision time for the teams who still don't have a satisfactory solution. They usually reason that paying for the solution is better than getting no solution or a poor solution. (Incidentally, the solution is on the answer page.)

Most students seem to enjoy this activity. It represents a change of pace from the normal routine and is a good experience for them.

PROGRESS REPORTS

Have you ever asked yourself any of the following questions?

- How am I doing in the classroom?
- Am I getting across to the students?
- Are they responding to my teaching strategies?
- Is there anything I can do that I am not doing to create a more effective learning environment and improve my classroom management skills?

These are questions many teachers ask themselves, especially during the beginning of their careers. If you have similar questions, you can attempt to answer them by giving students a teacher evaluation form or progress report to fill out. (See below.)

It is OK to do this at the end of the course and then read them, but consider the following. If you read the evaluations at the end of the course and realize that the students made suggestions that could have possibly improved the course, you can't do anything about it at this point. Some would argue that you could make changes for the next course; however, the next group of students will likely have different needs. Consequently, it seems that a better practice is to read the evaluations at the end of the first half of the course. Then you can consider implementing good suggestions during the second half.

Also, after reading the evaluations, it is probably effective to summarize the results and discuss them with the class. Students can then see how the class as a whole reacted and how many classmates responded the same way they did.

Progress reports can be a very effective tool. They provide you with firsthand knowledge of the views of the students and can aid in implementing changes to help create a more effective learning environment. Also, the students usually appreciate the opportunity to voice their opinions. This can help improve the rapport between you and the students and make classroom management a bit easier.

An example of a progress report is below.

Progress Report

Course_____

Period_____

Date_____

What I like *most* about this course is

What I like *least* about this course is

If I could ask the teacher to change *one* thing in this course it would be

Additional Comments

Thanks for your time and effort!

NEW YEAR'S RESOLUTION

Somewhat similar to the progress report is the "News Year's Resolution," which you can give to students the first day back from Christmas vacation. Included could be statements such as the following:

- One thing I can do to improve my performance in this class is . . .
- One thing the teacher can do to help me to improve my performance in this class is . . .

ASSIGNMENT SHEETS

Handing out assignment sheets to students at the beginning of a unit of work accomplishes several things:

- You don't have to announce an assignment every day. Tell students when the assignment sheets are first handed out that they will do one assignment per class unless you direct them to do otherwise.
- The students can work ahead. This is an important part of students working in groups. When they finish today's assignment, they can work on the next one.
- Absent students always have the assignment. You can post the assignment sheets on your web site or the school's web site. This ensures that students who miss class always have access to the homework.
- Parents can check the assignment sheet on the web site to monitor their child's homework.
- The test on each unit can be listed after the last assignment, so students cannot say, "I didn't know the test was today."

If you are not familiar with assignment sheets, a sample is below. At the bottom of each sheet you can include an inspirational message. Many of the suggested messages from the Message Game can be used here. (See Chapter 10.)

Algebra II, Chapter 7 Assignment Sheet

Note: Students are responsible for reading the corresponding textbook sections.

Section	Pages	Exercises
7.1	234–235	1–21 odd, 24, 26
7.2	239–240	2–30 even, 35

| 7.3 | 244–246 | 1, 2, 5, 7, 8, 10, 15, 26 |

Quiz: sections 7.1-7.3

7.4	250–251	1–10 all, 11–25 odd, 28
7.5	255–256	1–20
7.6	258–260	1–19 odd, 22, 26, 30
Review	265–268	1–30 (omit 22, 28), 32, 35

Test: Chapter 7

By failing to prepare, you are preparing to fail.

SELF-ESTEEM

Many adolescents have very little confidence about their abilities, especially in a math class. Is there anything you can do so that you do not lessen the self-esteem of a student when he or she is called on for an answer and the response is incorrect? In many cases, the answer is yes. Consider the following scenario.

Suppose the teacher, Ms. Cook, asks this question in an Algebra I class: "In general, what does the graph of a line with equation x = a constant look like?"

Jason is not a good math student and usually doesn't volunteer answers, so Ms. Cook is pleased to see him respond. Unfortunately, he says, "The graph is a horizontal line."

It took much courage for Jason to give this answer, and Ms. Cook doesn't want to discourage him from responding in the future. But he is wrong. Ms. Cook simply responds, "You're on the right track. If I had asked 'What does the graph of a line with equation y = a constant look like?' you would be 100% correct."

Jason reacts as if he had given the correct answer.

And this is what usually happens. Consequently, when a student gives a wrong answer, if possible you should make up a related question for which that answer is correct and tell the student that if that question had been asked, the answer would be correct. This procedure usually does not harm the student's self-esteem and encourages him or her to respond to questions in the future.

MONSTER MATH

The following is a group activity that clearly demonstrates that it is very difficult for a group to be successful unless every member does his or her job.

In this activity, each team of students is given the same four problems, all containing two parts. Teams must work quickly trying to arrive at the correct answer before the other teams do. One student cannot do all the problems and expect to finish before teams that shared the work. Each student must do his or her share.

In this particular activity, the correct solution to each problem results in an ordered pair of numbers. There are four such ordered pairs, which, when plotted on a piece of graph paper, constitute the four vertices of a quadrilateral. The objective of the team is to draw the diagonals of the quadrilateral and determine the point of intersection, which is the ultimate outcome being sought. Obviously, if one student gets the wrong coordinates of the vertex, the point of intersection will be incorrect. So each student has to know what he or she is doing in order for the team to be successful.

This activity is intended to be used around Halloween time in an algebra class, but it certainly can be modified and used in any class and any time of the year.

Below is a sample Monster Math activity. A blank format is also included. You can add your own problems, depending upon what part of the curriculum you are covering at this time of the year, or you can use problems previously done in the course and this exercise can serve as a review.

Monster Math: A Halloween Team Activity

Team Name _____

Period _____

It's Halloween night, and you are hanging out with some members of your math class. Suddenly, you become aware that there are monsters all around you! According to legend, you will be safe from the monsters if you can find the haunted house that is in this area (ironically, monsters are afraid of this haunted house). Each monster is at a point representing the vertex of a quadrilateral.

To find the coordinates of these points you must solve the four pairs of problems given below. Work in your team. Each team member does one (or more) of the problem sets. Plot all four points on graph paper, connect them to form a quadrilateral, and then draw the diagonals. The haunted house can be found at the point of intersection of the diagonals. Bring the graph of the quadrilateral and the correct coordinates of the point of intersection to me and you are safe. But you must hurry, for the haunted house has enough room for only three teams. If you don't find the haunted house in the next few minutes, then the monsters will find you!

1. Find the values of x and y. Plot the point (x,y) and call it M (for Mummy).

    $6x + 10 + 4x + 30 + 12x + 8 = 180$

    $3y + 17 = 4y - 4$

2. Find the values of x and y. Plot the point (x,y) and call it V (for Vampire).

    $2x - y = 16$

    $x + 2y = 68$

3. Find the values of x and y. Plot the point (x,y) and call it F (for Frankenstein's Monster).

    Four more than twice some number x is 40. Find x.

    $f(a) = 5a - 7$ $y = f(2)$ Find y.

4. Find the values of x and y. Plot the point (x,y) and call it W (for Werewolf).

    The *positive* root of $x^2 - 6x - 16 = 0$

    The *positive* root of $y^2 - 3y - 18 = 0$

Monster Math: A Halloween Team Activity

Team Name _____

Period _____

It's Halloween night, and you are hanging out with some members of your math class. Suddenly, you become aware that there are monsters all around you! According to legend, you will be safe from the monsters if you can find the haunted house that is in this area (ironically, monsters are afraid of this haunted house). Each monster is at a point representing the vertex of a quadrilateral.

To find the coordinates of these points you must solve the four pairs of problems given below. Work in your team. Each team member does one (or more) of the problem sets. Plot all four points on graph paper, connect them to form a quadrilateral, and then draw the diagonals. The haunted house can be found at the point of intersection of the diagonals. Bring the graph of the quadrilateral and the correct coordinates of the point of intersection to me and you are safe. But you must hurry, for the haunted house has enough room for only three teams. If you don't find the haunted house in the next few minutes, then the monsters will find you!

1. Find the values of x and y. Plot the point (x,y) and call it M (for Mummy).

2. Find the values of x and y. Plot the point (x,y) and call it V (for Vampire).

3. Find the values of x and y. Plot the point (x,y) and call it F (for Frankenstein's Monster).

4. Find the values of x and y. Plot the point (x,y) and call it W (for Werewolf).

THUMBS UP

At times while you are presenting material, you may be unclear as to whether or not the students are getting it. Looking at their faces is sometimes helpful, but many times the students have a blank expression (does this sound familiar?). At a time like this you can tell the students to give a thumbs-up gesture if they basically understand what is going on and a thumbs-down gesture if they don't. Ask them to make the gesture close to their chest so no one else can see it but you. Then at a quick glance you can determine about how many understand the material; the lesson can be adjusted accordingly.

As an alternative to the thumbs-up practice, you can ask the students to show you one finger if they understand the material, two fingers if they are not sure, and three fingers if they are lost. Emphasize that if they use one finger, make sure it is the index finger.

TEST TIME

Assessing student progress (testing) is obviously an important part of the learning process. It is amazing how many students don't know how to prepare for a test. Therefore, during the first few days of school give each student a copy of "Test-Taking Skills" (see below) or tell them it is posted on your web site. Tell them to read it carefully, and if they have questions they can be discussed in class. To increase the chances of their reading it, tell them that they will be given a quiz on test-taking skills in the near future. Wait a few days, and then give them the quiz shown below.

A copy of "Test-Taking Skills" should be available to parents, especially during parent conferences. Many parents feel powerless because they usually cannot help their children with the math; however, they can help them to prepare for a test by going over the suggestions covered in "Test-Taking Skills."

Test-Taking Skills

The following suggestions are intended to help you to be more successful when taking tests.

- Perhaps the most important aspect of taking a test is in the *preparation*. Consequently, be certain that you have attempted *all* the assignments pertaining to that test. Problems that caused you trouble should be dealt with as soon as possible, not the day before the test.
- Check over your work on the assignments to be sure you are able to do every type of problem. If not, seek help from the teacher, a tutor, or a classmate.
- A day or two before the test, make yourself a practice test, and include one of each type of basic problem from all the assignments leading up to the test. Take this practice test, giving yourself a time limit; this will help you to learn to work under the pressure of time.
- On the day of the test, come into class prepared with a pen or pencil, calculator, and other materials.
- When you first get the test, *read the directions* very carefully; for quick and easy reference, underline anything that is really important. While taking the test, you don't want to break your problem-solving thought process by stopping to read the directions or by asking the teacher a question that is already answered in the directions.
- Also, when you first receive the test, look it over completely, making mental or written notes as to which problems might be difficult or time consuming for you. If the order of solving the problems doesn't matter, do the easier problems first. Get as many problems done as possible before attacking the more difficult ones.
- Don't break your train of thought and waste time by asking the teacher inappropriate questions such as, "Am I doing this problem correctly?"
- Remember, virtually all tests have a time limit. You must learn to work quickly and accurately. Practicing working under the pressure of time (see the third item above) will help you during a test. Good luck!

Test-Taking Skills: Quiz

According to the sheet "Test-Taking Skills," classify each statement as true or false.

1. Perhaps the most important aspect of taking a test is in the *preparation*.
2. Prior to taking a test, be certain that you have attempted *all* the assignments pertaining to that test.
3. Problems that caused you trouble should be dealt with as soon as possible, not the day before the test.
4. A day or two before the test, make yourself a practice test; include one of each type of basic problems from all the assignments leading up to the test.
5. On the day of the test, come into class prepared with a pen or pencil, calculator, and other materials.
6. When you first get the test, *read the directions* very carefully; for quick and easy reference, underline anything that is really important.
7. When you first receive the test, look it over completely and then do the easier problems first.
8. Don't break your train of thought and waste time by asking the teacher inappropriate questions such as, "Am I doing this problem correctly?"
9. Take your time; there is no need to work quickly.
10. Wait until the last couple of hours before the test to study; that way the material will be fresh in your mind.

Another note about administrating tests: when the students are taking a test, you must be aware that some may attempt to "borrow" an answer from another student. It is wise to explain the penalty for cheating to students at the beginning of the course when you explain your ground rules and to repeat it before the first few tests. To reduce the chances of cheating, you should sit in the back of the room while administering the test. In this way the students don't know who you are watching. If you cough or clear your throat occasionally, this reminds them that you are observing them from the back of the room.

It is prudent to get up and walk around the room every 10 to 15 minutes. By glancing at each student's test, you can suggest to some students that they work more quickly if they are in danger of not completing the test before the period is over. While walking around you can also provide some encouragement to those who may need it or answer questions of a clarifying nature.

From the seated position or while walking around the room, if you observe a student looking at someone else's paper, don't make a big deal about it and embarrass the student. Have a file card available that has written on it the following:

Keep Your Eyes on Your Own Paper!

This Is the Only Warning You Will Get!

You can casually walk over to the student and flash him or her this card. That usually solves the problem. Keep a record of anyone warned, and if it happens again then the student can be severely penalized.

Speaking of cheating, an experienced math teacher tells the following story:

> One afternoon before leaving school, I was straightening out the desks in my room when I noticed someone had written the quadratic formula on the back of one of the chairs. The formula could be easily read by the person sitting directly behind that chair. Now, the students were required to memorize the formula for a quiz they were going to have the next day. Because I didn't actually see anyone write the formula on the back of the chair, and because there were eight classes in the room every day and the chairs are sometimes moved around, I could not accuse anyone of cheating. So what did I do? Did I erase the formula? No . . . I changed it!

Conclusion

In this book you have been exposed to many ideas, strategies, and materials. Now it is time to try using some of them in your lessons. However, keep in mind that it is difficult to successfully incorporate many new strategies or ideas over a short period of time. Remember, these concepts were developed and implemented over many years.

It is suggested that you choose an idea or strategy and try it with one class, preferably your best class. Tell them that you are going to try something new and that you would appreciate their input and honest, constructive criticism. Then do it. You may find that implementing an idea or strategy exactly the way it is presented in this book may not work for you. Consequently, you may want to make adjustments to fit your personality, teaching philosophy, and the needs of your students. Also, keep in mind that what works in your period-two class may not work in your period-three class. Successful teaching requires periodic analyzing and adjusting.

One of the great things about teaching is that if you try something and it doesn't go smoothly, you can analyze what happened, make the necessary adjustments, and try it again tomorrow, next week, next month, or next year.

You really won't know which strategies and ideas will work effectively for you until you try. If you slowly incorporate the concepts in this book that meet the needs of your students, you will likely improve your classroom management skills, and that's what this book and successful teaching are all about. *Good luck!*

Appendix

EXIT SLIP

Name_____

Class_____

Date_____

The most important thing(s) I learned in today's class:

Questions I have about today's class:

Before the next class I plan to . . .

Anything else?

COOPERATIVE LEARNING: GROUP PROCESSING

Groups need time to reflect on how well they are working together. They need to discuss what behaviors promote team harmony and which ones detract from it. These discussions, aided by group-processing forms, help the groups to function efficiently. Also, completing the forms guarantees that group members have the opportunity to express their opinions and receive feedback.

Through group processing, students can determine how well they are collaborating. Sometimes group processing can be very brief and require a minimum of time, while on other occasions it can be very thorough and time consuming. Whether brief or thorough, groups need to reflect on their effectiveness if cooperative learning is to be successful.

In the pages that follow, there are several models of group-processing forms. Some are to be completed by individual students, while others are to be completed by group members working together under the leadership of the taskmaster. If you are going to use groups in your classes, you are encouraged to use these or similar forms.

More forms are available online. You can use a search engine like Google and use the keywords, "cooperative learning, group processing forms." Exactly how these materials are used is up to you; however, it is suggested that simple forms are used first and, gradually, after students gain experience, more complex sheets are used.

Team Processing — Individual Evaluation: Form A

Circle the response that best represents how you interact in this team.

- I share my work and information with others in my group.

    YES   NO

- Others in my group share their work and information with me.

    YES   NO

- I support others in my group.

    YES   NO

- Others in my group support me.

    YES   NO

- In general, I work well with my group.

    YES   NO

COMMENTS:

_____

_____

_____

_____

_____

_____

_____

Team Processing—Individual Evaluation: Form B

Circle the number that best represents your participation in your team.

- I check to make sure everyone understands the directions.

    Poor   1   2   3   4   5   Excellent

- I share my materials and ideas.

    Poor   1   2   3   4   5   Excellent

- I am willing to give help.

    Poor   1   2   3   4   5   Excellent

- I encourage others to participate.

    Poor   1   2   3   4   5   Excellent

- I listen to others when they speak.

    Poor   1   2   3   4   5   Excellent

COMMENTS:

_____

_____

_____

_____

_____

_____

_____

Team Processing—Individual Evaluation: Form C

1. List things that you do in your team that help the team to work effectively.

_____
_____
_____
_____
_____
_____
_____

2. List things that you see that cause difficulties in your team.

_____
_____
_____
_____
_____
_____
_____

3. What can your team do to improve how well you work together?

_____
_____
_____
_____
_____
_____
_____

Team Processing—Team Evaluation: Form A

Under the leadership of the taskmaster, discuss each statement, and then circle the code that best describes your team's behavior. Use the following code:

- SA: *S*trongly *A*gree
- MA: *M*ostly *A*gree
- MD: *M*ostly *D*isagree
- SD: *S*trongly *D*isagree

1. We check to make sure we understand directions.

SA   MA   MD   SD

2. We give everyone the opportunity to express his or her point of view.

SA   MA   MD   SD

3. We listen without interrupting.

SA   MA   MD   SD

4. We help each other.

SA   MA   MD   SD

5. We support each other.

SA   MA   MD   SD

COMMENTS:

_____

_____

_____

_____

_____

_____

_____

Team Processing—Team Evaluation: Form B

Team Name _____

Date _____

Under the leadership of the taskmaster, discuss the statement, try to agree on your responses, and then write them in the spaces below.

- List three things we can do to help one another to learn in our teams:

  1. _____
  2. _____
  3. _____

- List three things we can do to improve group harmony:

  1. _____
  2. _____
  3. _____

- List three things the teacher can do to help to make our team more successful:

  1. _____
  2. _____
  3. _____

Signatures:

_____
_____
_____
_____
_____

Posttest Team Processing

Course_____

Period_____

Date_____

Team_____

Chapter/Topic_____

The taskmaster is expected to lead the discussion and to fill in the appropriate portion of this form. Upon completion, this paper is to be given to the teacher.

Did anyone in your team score *below* 70 on the last test? Circle one:

YES   NO

If you circled "Yes," complete part A only. If you circled "No," complete part B only.

A. As a team, list three things you can do in an attempt to get anyone who scored below 70 to improve future test scores (and, consequently, improve everyone's chances of earning extra credit).

1. _____
2. _____
3. _____

B. If everyone on your team scored 70 or better, list three things you did as a team that you feel contributed to your success.

1. _____
2. _____
3. _____

Taskmaster's Tasks

Taskmaster's Name _____

Period _____

Date _____

The primary duties of the taskmaster are to

1. help the team to focus on the task(s) at hand.
2. lead the team in determining which homework problems the team had trouble with.
3. accurately communicate the team's questions and concerns to the teacher.

Taskmaster's Tasks

Taskmaster's Name _____

Period _____

Date _____

The primary duties of the taskmaster are to

1. help the team to focus on the task(s) at hand.
2. lead the team in determining which homework problems the team had trouble with.
3. (accurately communicate the team's questions and concerns to the teacher.

Taskmaster Evaluation Form

Taskmaster's Name _____

Team Name _____

Period _____

Date _____

Circle the number that you feel is a fair evaluation of your taskmaster's performance on the given tasks. Our taskmaster

1. helps us to focus on the task at hand.

   Poor   1   2   3   4   5   Excellent

   Comments:

2. leads us in determining which homework problems the team had trouble with.

   Poor   1   2   3   4   5   Excellent

   Comments:

3. accurately communicates our questions and concerns to the teacher.

   Poor   1   2   3   4   5   Excellent

   Comments:

After completing this form, please give it to your taskmaster.

Team Report

Name	Weirdest Food You Have Eaten	Favorite T.V. Show	Farthest You Have Been From Home	Favorite Band	Favorite Sport's Team	Favorite Hobby or Activity	Favorite School Subject

What do the members of this team have in common?

What have you learned about your team?

Appendix

TEAM TOURNAMENT CHALLENGE SHEET

Name _____

Team _____

Question # ___ My challenge answer is _____
Question # ___ My challenge answer is _____
Question # ___ My challenge answer is _____
Question # ___ My challenge answer is _____
Question # ___ My challenge answer is _____
Question # ___ My challenge answer is _____
Question # ___ My challenge answer is _____
Question # ___ My challenge answer is _____
Question # ___ My challenge answer is _____
Question # ___ My challenge answer is _____
Question # ___ My challenge answer is _____
Question # ___ My challenge answer is _____
Question # ___ My challenge answer is _____
Question # ___ My challenge answer is _____
Question # ___ My challenge answer is _____
Question # ___ My challenge answer is _____
Question # ___ My challenge answer is _____
Question # ___ My challenge answer is _____
Question # ___ My challenge answer is _____
Question # ___ My challenge answer is _____

TEAM TOURNAMENT SCORECARD

Student Name	Team Name	Tally	Pts. Earned	Tournament Pts.

TEAM TOURNAMENT SCORECARD

Student Name	Team Name	Tally	Pts. Earned	Tournament Pts.

Appendix

SAMPLE TEAM TOURNAMENT SCORECARD

Student Name	Team Name	Tally	Pts. Earned	Tournament Pts.
Babe	A	IIIIII	6	5
Lou	B	III	3	2
Joe	C	IIIII	5	4
Mickey	D	IIIIIIIII	9	6
Derek	E	IIIII	5	4
Reggie	F	II	2	1

Above is a scorecard from *one* of four large groups of students.

Team A	*Team B*	*Team C*	*Team D*	*Team E*	*Team F*
Babe 5	Lou 2	Joe 4	Mickey 6	Derek 4	Reggie 1
2	1	5	1	5	2
3	6	5	3	2	6
1	4	2	2		
Totals 11	13	16	12	11	9

Scores that do not have names next to them represent students in other groups and on other scorecards.

Dividing the above totals by 4, 4, 4, 4, 3, and 3 respectively (the number of members of each team) results in the final team scores of 2.75, 3.25, 4.0, 3.0, 3.67, and 3.0. The final results are as follows:

- First place: Team C
- Second place: Team E
- Third Place: Team B

1	2	3	4	5	6	7
8	9	10	11	12	13	14
15	16	17	18	19	20	21
22	23	24	25	26	27	28
29	30	31	32	33	34	35
36	37	38	39	40	41	42
43	44	45	46	47	48	49
50	51	52	53	54	55	56
57	58	59	60	TRIPLE POINT VALUE	DOUBLE POINT VALUE	DOUBLE POINT VALUE

Answers to Selected Exercises

What Comes Next?

1. 21 (add 4)
2. 3 (subtract 3)
3. 1/16 (divide by 2)
4. 11 (add 1, then 2, then 3, etc.)
5. 8 (Fibonacci sequence; add the previous two numbers)
6. M (May; months))
7. T (Thursday; days of the week)
8. F (Fifth; ordinal numbers)
9. S (So; musical scale)
10. Varies: 3, if the sequence is the natural numbers; 4, if the previous number is being doubled; 1, if the sequence is 1, 2, 1, 2, 1, 2, . . . This problem illustrates that it is not wise to jump to conclusions based on a limited amount of data. This problem could lead into a discussion of prejudice.

Challenge: If we assign a number value to each letter with A = 1, B = 2, C = 3, and so forth, then the sequence becomes 16, 25, 36, 49, 64. These numbers are the squares of 4, 5, 6, 7, and 8, respectively. Consequently, the missing entry must represent the square of 9, or 81, which means *HA* is the missing term.

The Bottom Line

Solution: $3 - 4 \times 9 = 3 - 36 = -33$

Up in Smoke

103 days

Five-a-Day Is the Healthy Way

911

The Witch's Broom

The broom costs $15.

The North Pole

100 miles (Remember, the earth is a sphere.)

Sick Leave

Walter was a newborn baby.

A Riddle

Charcoal

Coins, Coins, Coins

45 pennies, 2 nickels, 2 dimes, and 1 quarter

Equations Investigations

1. Letters of the Alphabet
2. Signs of the Zodiac
3. Degrees Fahrenheit at which Water Freezes
4. Degrees in a Right Angle
5. Hours in a Day
6. Days in February in a Leap Year
7. Days and Nights of the Great Flood
8. Days Has September, April, June, and November
9. Wise Men
10. Dwarfs

CHAPTER 5: INQUIRY-BASED AND DISCOVERY LESSONS

Checkerboard Squares

In total there are 204 squares on a checkerboard.

Parabolas from Data

1. $y = x^2 + 2x$
2. $y = x^2 - 2x + 3; (1, 2)$
3. $y = x^2 - 4x + 7; (2, 3)$
4. $y = 2x^2 - 4x + 3; (1, 1)$
5. $y = 2x^2 - x + 4; (1/4, 31/8)$

End Behavior

1. up, up
2. up, down
3. down, down
4. up, up
5. down, up
6. up, down
7. down, down
8. down, up
9. up, up
10. up, down

Conclusions:

If $a > 0$, n even: up, up
If $a < 0$, n even: down, down
If $a > 0$, n odd: down, up
If $a < 0$, n odd: up, down

CHAPTER 8: THE GRAPHING CALCULATOR

Bones, Bones, Bones

Answers may vary depending on the particular class from which the data is taken, but it is most likely the tibia found belonged to Bernie Boots.

CHAPTER 12: BUT WAIT . . . THERE'S MORE

The Consultant/Water Consumption

Volume of pool = 2036 ft.^{3}
90% of volume = 1832 ft.^{3}
Current usage: 3200 ft.^{3}
Previous usage: 1400 ft.^{3}
Difference: 1800 ft.^{3}
The refilling of the pool could account for the increased water consumption.

Monster Math

M: (6, 21); *V*: (20, 24); *F*: (18, 3); *W*: (8, 6); Point of intersection: (12, 12)

Test-Taking Skills: Quiz

All answers are true except numbers 9 and 10.

About the Author

Nicholas J. Rinaldi has more than four decades of experience teaching mathematics at the high school level. He has also taught "Math Strategies in Secondary Education," a university graduate course in education for students preparing to be math teachers at the secondary or middle school levels.

Printed in Great Britain
by Amazon.co.uk, Ltd.,
Marston Gate.